Clearing, Settlement and Custody

DATE DUE

1-22-04 JAN 2 0 2004	

Butterworth-Heinemann – The Securities Institute
A publishing partnership

About The Securities Institute

Formed in 1992 with the support of the Bank of England, the London Stock Exchange, the Financial Services Authority, LIFFE and other leading financial organizations, the Securities Institute is the professional body for practitioners working in securities, investment management, corporate finance, derivatives and related businesses. Their purpose is to set and maintain professional standards through membership, qualifications, training and continuing learning and publications. The Institute promotes excellence in matters of integrity, ethics and competence.

About the series

Butterworth-Heinemann is pleased to be the official **Publishing Partner** of the Securities Institute with the development of professional level books for: Brokers/Traders; Actuaries; Consultants; Asset Managers; Regulators; Central Bankers; Treasury Officials; Compliance Officers; Legal Departments; Corporate Treasurers; Operations Managers; Portfolio Managers; Investment Bankers; Hedge Fund Managers; Investment Managers; Analysts and Internal Auditors, in the areas of: Portfolio Management; Advanced Investment Management; Investment Management Models; Financial Analysis; Risk Analysis and Management; Capital Markets; Bonds; Gilts; Swaps; Repos; Futures; Options; Foreign Exchange; Treasury Operations.

Series titles

■ **Professional Reference Series**
  The Bond and Money Markets: *Strategy, Trading, Analysis*

■ **Global Capital Markets Series**
  The REPO Handbook
  Foreign Exchange and Money Markets: *Theory, Practice and Risk Management*
  IPO and Equity Offerings
  European Securities Markets Infrastructure
  Best Execution in the Integrated Securities Market

■ **Operations Management Series**
  Clearing, Settlement and Custody
  Controls, Procedures and Risks
  Relationship and Resource Management in Operations
  Managing Technology in the Operations Function
  Regulation and Compliance in Operations
  Understanding the Markets

For more information

For more information on **The Securities Institute** please visit their web site:

www.securities-institute.org.uk

and for details of all **Butterworth-Heinemann Finance** titles please visit Butterworth-Heinemann:

www.bh.com/finance

Clearing, Settlement and Custody

David Loader

BUTTERWORTH
HEINEMANN

OXFORD   AMSTERDAM   BOSTON   LONDON   NEW YORK   PARIS
SAN DIEGO   SAN FRANCISCO   SINGAPORE   SYDNEY   TOKYO

Butterworth-Heinemann
An imprint of Elsevier Science
Linacre House, Jordan Hill, Oxford OX2 8DP
225 Wildwood Avenue, Woburn, MA 01801-2041

First published 2002

British Library Cataloguing in Publication Data
A catalogue record for this book is available from the British Library

Library of Congress Cataloguing in Publication Data
A catalogue record for this book is available from the Library of Congress

ISBN 0 7506 5465 1

For information on all Butterworth-Heinemann finance publications
visit our website at: www.bh.com/finance

Composition by Genesis Typesetting, Rochester, Kent
Printed and bound in Great Britain by Biddles Ltd, *www.biddles.co.uk*

Contents

Preface

Clearing, settlement and custody is an enormous subject that is at the heart of everything that happens in the financial markets. Today the clearing and settlement process is, in many cases, highly automated and yet sometimes there is still the traditional certificate as evidence of ownership and manual processes to clear and settle transactions in the marketplace. The evolution of clearing and settlement is one that is still happening and as such it is impacting on the operations function through both new practices but also increasingly in terms of regulation, risk and reputation.

Until the mid-1990s the issue of clearing and settlement revolved around issues like constraints on business, problems with delayed settlement, dematerialization of settlement and cross-border settlement. The whole focus and image of clearing and settlement was really about administration and there was plenty to focus on. However, the events surrounding a bank operating in derivatives products in Singapore was to change the whole concept of clearing and settlement for ever.

The ultimate collapse of Barings Bank was not the result of a single failure or a single act by an individual, but rather a combination of situations and failures in management. What was certain, however, was that there were issues related to operations that hitherto had been considered to be inefficiencies and that would now be recognized as risk.

Clearing and settlement is a process, one that takes a transaction to its ultimate conclusion and provided that the details of that transaction are agreed, monitored, reconciled and reported, any business will be relatively safe from unexpected losses or problems. If, on the other hand, that process is running in an uncontrolled way then there is a risk that it will become unable to protect the business from malpractice and errors elsewhere and in particular in its trading activity.

Operational risk became part of risk management and operations risk became part of clearing and settlement.

In essence, though, the efficient clearing and settlement operation is managing risk, not because it is a direct part of the process but more that it is a by-product. The routine procedures relate to reconciliation and record-keeping. If these are performed efficiently and accurately it will result in accurate records of activity and profit/loss.

The settlement process involves the clearing house and clearing broker, the non-clearing broker and/or the client. Each is to some extent dependent on the performance of the next and previous part of the chain. The timings and deadlines for information and instructions is a crucial part of the overall process and has many implications for managers in operations.

The routine settlement process involves various stages originating from actions on trade day and after at the clearing house and possibly the custodian. Issues that arise include:

- Source of trade data, trade input and trade matching
- This will be an automatic process on electronic markets but not on other markets
- On open-outcry markets the process will involve trade tickets, manual trade input, trade matching and error resolution
- Once the trade matching is complete the details pass to the clearing house

- On some exchanges the process of acceptance of trades is made via computer links between members and the exchange/clearing house
- The trade is booked to either a house or client account where segregated positions are maintained by the brokers and many of the clearing houses
- Certain events will occur like corporate actions, close-out of positions and any exercise/delivery notices being submitted for derivatives
- Trade details, positions etc. are on some markets available to the clearing members real time

Then we have other scenarios that occur after the trade day

- Clearing house provides settlement details, including for derivatives any delivery exercise or assignment details
- At the designated time the settlement is fulfilled by the clearing house or member through the prescribed method
- Failure to meet the settlement requirement in a central clearing counterparty market can result in the member being placed in default

There are obviously many settlement issues for managers and there are key issues arising from the routine settlement functions including the accuracy and timeliness of:

- Accounts records and records keeping
- Reconciliation of positions, cash and collateral
- Settlement of any liabilities with the clearing house and clients
- Regulatory reporting

The manager must ensure that robust procedures and controls are in place for each of these processes and procedures. Procedures and controls need to cover:

- Booking instructions – *source and verification, escalation route for problems*
- Settlement fails – *source and action to resolve*

- Close-outs – *submission of instruction and verification*
- Exercise/assignment and delivery tender – *source of instruction, verification, timing of submission, correct method, verification of action being completed*
- Position and cash reconciliation – *frequency and sign-off, completion prior to trading next day*
- Settlement with clearing house – *management of process, funding and asset availability, timing*

Many of these tasks are ongoing throughout the day and are subject to various influences including:

- Source and timing of receipt of transaction data from dealers/clients
- Reconciliation and confirmation of acceptance of data to market/clearing house within exchange deadlines
- Variable volumes of activity
- Treasury management
- Margin and collateral management

The procedures will also need to include the escalation route for any disputes or problems so that at all times the operations team are able to meet the deadlines imposed by the exchanges and clearing houses, central securities depositories, agents, custodians etc. This is important not simply from an efficiency point of view but also in risk management terms.

The settlement process is a key element in identifying and correcting errors made by dealers and traders. Failure to identify the error or act promptly will result in potentially serious financial loss as well as worrying audit and the regulators.

Given that we are also undergoing a massive rationalization of the structure of clearing and settlement in the industry and seeking twin goals of automation and shortening settlement cycles, the challenge for operations managers is considerable; it is also very clear.

Manage costs, eradicate inefficiencies, create the environment to be competitive and implement the procedures to meet the future changes that will occur.

In this book we explore clearing and settlement by looking at some of the different roles, the processes and procedures and the key issues.

Chapter 1

The structure of clearing and settlement

What is clearing and settlement? An interesting question and one that, on the face of it, could be answered by a simple definition and yet in the financial markets it is often a very little understood but vital process.

For every transaction that takes place in the markets there is a process that concludes the transaction. In general terms that will mean some kind of exchange taking place between the two parties to the trade. The exchange may be cash for a security or the netted outcome of more than one transaction, for instance the end result of a purchase and sale.

Clearing is a term that is easily associated with banking so that we have the 'clearing banks'. In this instance the item being 'cleared' is money and, historically, cheques. When a cheque is drawn it has a value that is only realized when the receiving bank has presented it to the drawing bank and received the value, hence the term 'value date'. As most people know, the time to obtain the value may be three or even more days from the paying into the account of the cheque. Today the somewhat antiquated process of cheques being cleared has been partially replaced by automated processes or electronic banking and yet in many cases the time before value is obtained is still several days!

In the financial markets there is not only cash but also money market instruments like Treasury bills. A transaction in these bills is settled in the UK through the Central Money Market Office (CMO) a function that is run through CREST. CREST is the UK securities settlement service for both money market instruments and also UK and international securities and bonds. This includes equities, bonds, unit trusts and shares in open-ended investment companies (OEICs).

So money is cleared and settled and so are securities as well as commodities and derivatives, although the processes may be very different.

The process of clearing can be defined as:

> **The preparation through matching, recording and processing instructions of a transaction for settlement**

Settlement can be defined as:

> **The exchange of cash or assets in return for other assets or cash and transference of the ownership of those assets and cash**

In each market around the world transactions in financial market instruments follow the same basic principle of clearing and settlement. The process of clearing and settlement is often linked with another process, the holding of securities. When this occurs we find central securities depositories or CSDs for short. CSDs hold securities centrally on behalf of their members to speed the process of clearing and settlement, the selling party does not have to send the securities to the buying party who may be resident overseas. This also helps to reduce the possibility of the loss of securities. This is, of course, extremely important in the case of bearer securities where there is no evidence of ownership recorded.

It is important to note that the clearing process is carried out by a designated function, and the organization that performs this function is often called a clearing house. The clearing house operates either completely or to a significant degree independently of the exchanges, market or markets its serves. The responsibility for managing and overseeing the trading process is therefore quite separate from the process of controlling the transactions through to settlement. The clearing house does not make the rules and regulations pertaining to carrying out transactions but it does establish the rules, in conjunction with the regulator and the exchange, by which its members will clear and settle the business.

Figures 1.1 and 1.2 show the financial market structure in the UK and the United States as given in the excellent International Securities Services Association handbook.

Today, as with so much of the financial markets, change is taking place in the way in which activity on markets is cleared and settled.

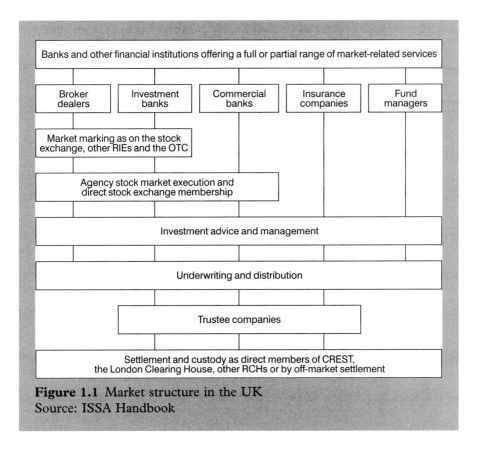

Figure 1.1 Market structure in the UK
Source: ISSA Handbook

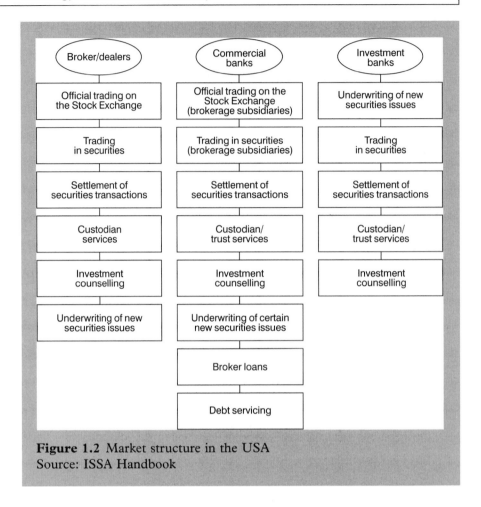

Figure 1.2 Market structure in the USA
Source: ISSA Handbook

The central clearing counterparty (CCP), essentially a process of not just facilitating settlement but guaranteeing it, is becoming common in securities markets and thus the clearing and settlement of securities is moving towards the same process as that used for derivatives.

In the UK, the London Clearing House (LCH), a major clearer of derivatives for many years, joined with CREST to provide a central clearing process for equities called EquityClear. Figure 1.3 shows the relationship between parties prior to EquityClear.

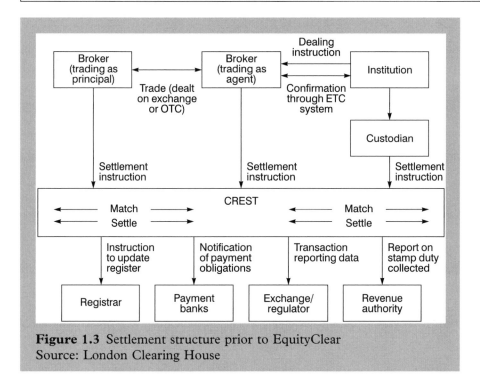

Figure 1.3 Settlement structure prior to EquityClear
Source: London Clearing House

Figure 1.4 shows the possible relationships between the trading, clearing and settlement roles with the CCP. Note that there need not necessarily be a one-to-one relationship between the trading member as legal entity and either the clearing member or the settlement entity.

We look at the CCP in more detail later in the book but it is important to remember that the changes in clearing and settlement are impacting on operations teams and, of course, the procedures and controls they use. There are many benefits, as we shall see, of the CCP but also a need to ensure that firms and clients are aware of what the changes mean to long-established procedures.

We also need to focus on the fact that clearing and settlement processes in different markets are covered by local conventions and in

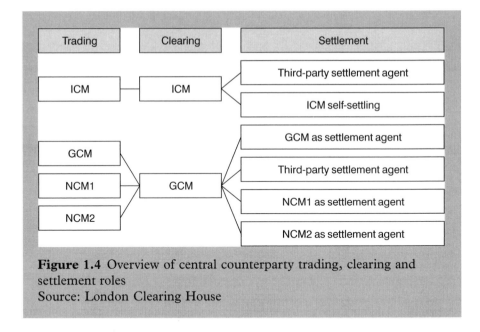

Figure 1.4 Overview of central counterparty trading, clearing and settlement roles
Source: London Clearing House

turn these differ sometimes considerably from jurisdiction to jurisdiction and also from one product to another.

The introduction of many initiatives over the years has led to a more streamlined process and yet one that is by no means uniform across countries. These initiatives include those set out by the Group of 30, an industry body made regarding issues surrounding the settlement of securities in the late 1980s. The International Securities Services Association (ISSA) later took on board the recommendations that they made, updated them and monitored markets to ascertain the extent of their implementation. Today we see many of the recommendations as standard practice in most, but not all, markets. Times have changed, and ISSA issued more recommendations in 2000 that sought to build on those of G30 and improve the whole settlement environment from the angles of both efficiency and risk. It is worth looking at the G30 and ISSA 2000 Recommendations and the key points follow.

Group of 30 recommendations

1 All comparisons of trades between direct market participants (i.e. brokers, broker dealers and other exchange members) should be accomplished by T+0. Matched trade details should be linked to the settlement system.

2 Indirect market participants (such as institutional investors, and other indirect trading counterparties) should achieve positive affirmation of trade details on T+1.

3 Each country should have in place an effective and fully developed central securities depository, organized and managed to encourage the broadest possible direct and indirect industry participation. The range of depository eligible instruments should be as wide as possible. Immobilization or dematerialization of financial instruments should be achieved to the utmost extent possible.

4 Each market is encouraged to reduce settlement risk by introducing either Real Time Gross Settlement or a trade netting system that fully meets the 'Lamfalussy Recommendations'.

5 Delivery versus payment (DVP) should be employed as the method for settling all securities transactions. DVP is defined as simultaneous, irrevocable and immediately available exchange of securities and cash on a continuous basis throughout the day.

6 Payments associated with the settlement of securities transactions and the servicing of securities portfolios should be made consistent across all instruments and markets by adopting the 'same day' funds convention.

7 A rolling settlement system should be adopted by all markets. Final settlement for all trades should occur no later than T+3.

8 Securities lending and borrowing should be encouraged as a method of expediting the settlement of securities transaction. Existing regulatory and taxation barriers that inhibit the practice of lending securities should be removed.

9 Each country should adopt the standard for securities messages developed by the International Organization of Standardization (ISO Standard 7775). In particular, countries should adopt the ISIN numbering system for securities issues as defined in the ISO Standard 6166.

Source: Clearance & Settlement Systems in the World's Securities Markets, G30 (1989) and updated by ISSA (May 1995).

Insight

The key points of the ISSA 2000 Recommendations

1 Securities systems have a primary responsibility to their users and other stakeholders. They must provide effective low-cost processing. Services should be priced equitably.

2 Securities systems must allow the option of network access on an interactive basis. They should cope with peak capacity without any services degradation, and have sufficient standby capabilities to recover operations in a reasonably short period within each processing day.

3 The industry worldwide must satisfy the need for efficient, fast settlement by full adherence to the International Securities Numbering process (ISO 6166) and uniform usage of ISO 15022 standards for all securities messages. The industry should seek to introduce a global client and counterparty identification methodology (BIC – ISO 9362) to further facilitate straightthrough processing. Applications and programmes should be structured in such a way as to facilitate open interaction between all parties.

4 Each market must have clear rules ensuring investor protection by safeguarding participants from the financial risks of failed settlement and that listed companies are required to follow sound policies on corporate governance, transfer of economic benefits and shareholder rights.

5 The major risks in securities systems should be mitigated by five key measures, namely:

- The implementation of real delivery versus payment
- The adoption of a trade date plus one settlement cycle in a form that does not increase operational risk
- The minimization of funding and liquidity constraints by enabling stock lending and borrowing, broad based cross-collateralization, the use of repos and netting as appropriate
- The enforcement of scripless settlement
- The establishment of mandatory trade matching and settlement performance measures

6 Convergence of securities systems, both within countries and across borders, should be encouraged where this eliminates operational risk, reduces cost and enhances market efficiency.

7 Investor compliance with the laws and regulations in the home countries of their investments should be part of their regulators' due diligence process. Investors, in turn, should be treated equitably in the home country of their investments especially in respect to their rights to shareholder benefits and concessionary arrangements under double-tax agreements.

8 Local laws and regulations should ensure that there is segregation of client assets from the principal assets of their custodian; and no possible claim on client assets in the event of custodian bankruptcy or a similar occurrence. Regulators and markets, to further improve investor protection, should work:

- To ensure clarity on the applicable law on cross-border transactions
- To seek international agreement on a legally enforceable definition of finality in a securities transaction
- To ensure that local law fully protects the rights of beneficial owners
- To strengthen securities laws to secure both the rights of the pledgee and the protection accorded to client assets held in securities systems

It is readily apparent from these recommendations that certain issues pertaining to clearing and settlement did, and in some cases still do, have a significant impact on the efficiency of the process, and therefore the efficiency of the market as a whole.

In later chapters we look at issues like delivery versus payment, netting and stock lending but from the recommendations we can see that where these facilities are not available or not used the overall settlement process is likely to be at a higher level of risk. We need to be clear, however, that, for instance, the absence of stock lending does not mean that trades will fail to settle on the due settlement date. What it does mean is that certain activities like market-making where the trader can sell short in the market, i.e. the trader does not own the stock they have just sold, would be severely curtailed if the ability to borrow stock to settle short sales was not possible. That in turn would potentially affect liquidity in the particular security and perversely probably cause settlement problems.

The G30 and ISSA recommendations, and indeed those of other industry organizations and representative bodies, are designed to improve the clearing and settlement process. The improvement to the process may take time and may also create a period of increased difficulties for organizations before the benefits take effect. What is vital is that operations managers and teams are alert to the need not only to react efficiently to these recommendations but to also actively participate in their design and implementation.

The clearing and settlement conventions we find in countries today are a mix of regulatory driven, traditional market practices and participant driven.

The current convention in the UK market is an example of how change has affected the process and that some of that change needed regulatory approval or a change to the law.

Settlement in the UK was on a period basis such that a Stock Exchange Account Period of ten business days existed. All trades carried out in that period would settle on an 'Account Day' a week later. Settlement was by scrip or paper, in either registered or bearer form and in the case of registered securities required the completion of a transfer form to accompany the registered certificate.

The change to dematerialized settlement by electronic book entry recording of securities as per the G30 Recommendation 3 required not only the introduction of a central system for settlement but also the permission of shareholders of companies whose securities would be settled in dematerialized form. Such was the concern of brokers operating for private clients at the loss of the certificate as evidence of ownership that they successfully lobbied the authorities for retention of the option to have a security settled in certificated form. In most other countries where dematerialized settlement now exists it is the only permitted format. The dual capability in the UK is going to cause problems at some stage in the future as other significant initiatives begin to happen, one such initiative being the move to a settlement convention of trade day+1(T+1). It will be almost impossible for the settlement to take place one day after the trade where a physical certificate is required to effect the settlement, e.g. the transfer of ownership.

To summarize the structure of clearing and settlement that we have covered so far we know that:

- Clearing is the preparation of a transaction for settlement
- Settlement is the exchange of assets and cash as well as legal ownership
- Clearing houses and central securities depositories provide the clearing, settlement and securities depository functions to the markets
- This function covers securities such as equities, bonds, money markets, derivatives, commodities and cash
- Clearing and settlement takes place under the conventions currently applicable to the country, market and product
- Industry bodies make recommendations to improve the efficiency and risk management of securities settlement

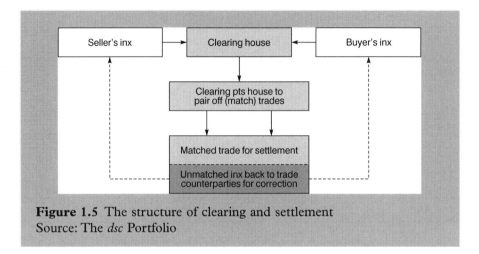

Figure 1.5 The structure of clearing and settlement
Source: The *dsc* Portfolio

So far we have looked at the structure of clearing and settlement focusing on the relationship between the exchange, the clearing and the settlement process through the matching of trades, and resolution of unmatched trades, prior to settlement as implied by Figure 1.5.

It is interesting to look at the objectives and mission statements as stated by a selection of different clearing organizations.

Insight

The Government Securities Clearing Corporation (United States)
The Government Securities Clearing Corporation (GSCC) is an industry service organization, designed to operate on a not-for-profit basis, whose primary purpose is to ensure orderly settlement in the government securities marketplace. It serves to bring both operational and risk management benefits to the clearance and settlement of government securities through the provision of automated trade comparison, netting, and settlement services for the US government securities marketplace. GSCC's automated system is designed to provide real-time interactive communication facilities for the clearance and settlement of government debt products.

Insight

The London Clearing House (United Kingdom)
The overall objective of the London Clearing House (LCH) is to provide secure and efficient clearing services to its members, protecting the integrity of the underlying markets, both exchange-traded and over-the-counter. LCH will maintain its position as the premier central counterparty in the European time zone – independent of trading platform and settlement organization – and will seek to link its business with similarly structured clearing houses in other time zones.

Insight

The Depository Trust and Clearing Corporation (United States)
Facing accelerated change and new challenges in the financial services field, the National Securities Clearing Corporation (NSCC) and the Depository Trust Company (DTC) agreed to an integration approved by the Securities and Exchange Commission on 13 September 1999. The plan called for a holding company, The Depository Trust and Clearing Corporation (DTCC) with two separate operating subsidiaries, an executive management team and a single slate of directors. DTC and NSCC were both established in the mid-1970s in response to the 'paperwork crisis' that had been affecting the securities industry since the late 1960s and, for a while, forced the country's major stock exchanges to close one day a week in order to process the backlog of paperwork. Unable to keep pace with the rising volume in trading, the securities industry established the two companies to accelerate post-trade processing and reduce risk.

The goal of integration is to prepare for the future, to leverage the respective strengths of NSCC and DTC and to create an organization that can support the changing financial services business in the USA and overseas. The core capabilities of its subsidiaries are:

- Electronic post-trade processing for institutional and broker-to-broker trades
- Risk management assessment and surveillance programmes
- Cash netting and settlement
- Custody/asset-servicing
- High-volume communications network management
- High-capacity data centre management, including failsafe capabilities

Insight

Euroclear (International)

The Euroclear System is the world's largest clearance and settlement system for internationally traded securities. It has been instrumental in the development of the international securities markets, serving as a catalyst for higher settlement efficiency and risk control.

Serving as the premier provider of cross-border securities services, the Euroclear System has about 2000 participants worldwide. The majority are banks, broker/dealers, custodians, and other institutions professionally engaged in managing new issues of securities, market-making, trading, or holding the wide variety of securities accepted in the system.

Clearstream (International)

Clearstream International is a leading clearing and settlement organization for both domestic and cross-border bonds, equities and investment funds. They have over 2500 customers in 80 locations worldwide and they perform many roles in support of the diverse and complex industry they operate in. Clearstream is a settlement agent and custodian bank that settles over 500 000 transactions per day in over 200 000 securities. As a back-office specialist it has a full range of insourcing capabilities for securities administration and cash clearing. It efficiently performs the daily operational and monitoring functions required for securities lending and borrowing and can also act as the agent for both borrower and lender in securities lending transactions.

Sources: adapted from the websites of the organizations

From the above we can see how the organizations differ and yet in general terms are involved in the same process. Clearing, settlement, custody, payments and risk management are all services that form part or all of the function of these organizations. Often there is little to choose between them. For instance, Table 1.1 shows some examples of the services offered by CRESTCo, Euroclear and Clearstream.

We will look at various aspects of clearing and settlement in more detail as we move through the book, however, it is also important to look at clearing and settlement not just from the process point of view but also from the business angle.

Clearing and settlement is a necessity but it is also a cost. That cost can be significantly higher than it need be because of the inefficiency of the operations teams in banks, brokers and institutional clients.

Table 1.1 Services offered by clearing organizations

CRESTCo	Euroclear	Clearstream
Real-time Securities Settlement Services Operates in real time, settling large volumes of transactions at low cost and in multiple currencies, allowing customers to monitor their transactions throughout process	Real-time settlement platform The only platform able to settle cross-border bond and equity transactions from all European and other major markets in real time	Real-time settlement Fully automated overnight and daytime processing across the Creation Platform provides real-time communication with a global network of correspondent and depository banks
Portfolio of settlement services includes, gilts, unit trusts and shares in open-ended investment companies (OEICs) and money market instruments (CMO)	Users of the real-time settlement platform benefit by being able to manage their trades with greater flexibility and less exposure to risk	The infrastructure ensures accurate handling of transactions in all types of securities and a wide range of currencies
CRESTCo is not a profit-maximizing organization, its charges are among the lowest of comparable settlement systems	Overnight batch settlement – takes place during the night prior to the relevant value date for settlement	Clearstream Banking – offers customers a network of top-rated depository banks which provide a wide range of custody-related services: ■ Securities events ■ Income and redemption processing ■ Withholding tax service ■ Proxy voting
	Euroclear participants have access to comprehensive custody services	Clearstream Banking custody services help reduce the administrative burden connected with any corporate actions associated with securities positions held in customer accounts
	Integrated Collateral Management – main benefit is for Euroclear participants to optimize use of the assets they hold in the Euroclear System with the greatest flexibility	

Note: the above information has been taken from the websites of the three clearing organizations.

Some of the cost is, of course, core cost set by the fees charged by CSDs and clearing houses. Those fees vary and often cross-border settlement is more expensive than domestic settlement because of the duplication of fees levied by the clearers involved. However, some settlement cost is nothing to do with the clearing organizations but is the cost incurred by the administration, safekeeping and sundry other functions and processes that are involved in the pre- and post-settlement environments.

The cost of developing a capability to handle some or all of these functions can be onerous such that for many organizations it is cheaper and more efficient to utilize the services of specialist providers. Into this category fall organizations offering custody, derivative clearing and fund administration. More recently the outsourcing of almost the entire operations function has become a possibility as prime brokers and other similar organizations seek to utilize their own in-house functionality more efficiently by gaining revenue from other organizations reluctant to commit to the expense of developing systems and people to meet ever more onerous regulatory and competitive requirements as well as more and more complex products, trading and investment strategies.

To illustrate just how significant the costs and the risk can be we can look at how the number of banks offering custodian services has shrunk. Today many large banks are no longer offering custody to third parties and some do not even run the capability for themselves, preferring to utilize the services offered by the larger CSDs and international CSDs like Euroclear and Clearstream, who today offer custody services alongside their clearing and settlement services.

As technology and changes to settlement practices speed up the processes and real-time settlement in a straight through processing environment creates the need for sophisticated systems solutions to provide ever more complex services in-house and to clients, it is little wonder that the cost of clearing and settlement is becoming more and more of an issue for most organizations.

As a result the securities financing facilities that are offered and utilized are extremely important. Facilities like stock lending, repurchase agreements (repos) and collateral provision are utilized to generate additional income from securities. On the same principle, the CSDs and custodians recognize that the efficient and timely collection of income and benefits from securities held in a portfolio are important in the overall cost of the business equation and accordingly offer added-value services to achieve this for clients.

Thus the structure of clearing and settlement is very much a core activity concerning the matching and settlement of trades complemented by a range of services allied to these two functions. The clearing function can be independent from or part of an exchange or exchanges. Not surprisingly, the various clearers have their own industry bodies of which they are members. Organizations such as the European Central Securities Depository Association (ECSDA) and the Asia Pacific Central Securities Depository Association (APSCDA) are an example.

One thing that is certain with the structure of clearing and settlement is that it will undergo considerable change over the coming months and years. In the next chapter we look at the role of the clearing houses and central securities depositories, and later the custodians.

Chapter 2

The role of the clearing house and central securities depositories

In Chapter 1 we determined that whenever a trade takes place in the financial markets there is an associated settlement process. That process involves several procedures ranging from matching to settlement instructions being actioned. We also saw that clearing therefore can be described as the process of matching and recording transactions prior to the settlement of those transactions. A clearing house is the organization that deals with the logistics of this process and while it is often part of the exchange itself it provides an element of independence from the exchange. The clearing function is a crucial one in terms of risk management and credibility for the exchange. It provides the mechanism for monitoring the trades and, where the clearing organization is providing a central counterparty clearing facility, a guarantee to the buying and selling counterparty removing that particular counterparty risk.

An exchange needs to establish a clearing house so that the trades executed by its members are routed successfully towards final settlement within the conventions for the product and market. Figure 2.1 shows the generic flow for a securities transaction.

The London Clearing House (LCH) and CREST are providing the clearing process for transactions in London but each has a different role in that process. CREST is providing the matching and settlement facility to its members for securities traded and LCH is

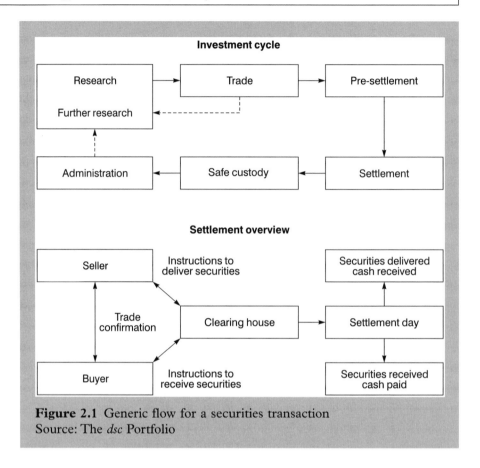

Figure 2.1 Generic flow for a securities transaction
Source: The *dsc* Portfolio

providing the central clearing counterparty facility for derivatives, and now also to CREST for securities trades.

The history of the London Clearing House is interesting, as it provides us with an insight into the development of the clearing process. The forerunner of LCH was the International Commodities Clearing House (ICCH), an organization that, as its name implies, historically cleared commodities traded on many markets around the world. The clearing process was principally aimed at:

- Ensuring contracts entered into would be honoured
- Guaranteeing that the quality of the commodity was to the standard set by the clearing house

■ Providing rules and regulations for the trading, settlement and delivery of the commodities

As part of this process the ICCH became the guarantor of the contract traded and charged a margin as a deposit to ensure that obligations were honoured. So successful was this concept that when member defaults through a failure to meet their obligations occurred the clearing house was able to manage the situation without losses to other members. The clearing process for commodities and derivatives is clearly a proven one and, as this process is adopted into other markets, operations teams will benefit in several ways, not least the reduction of settlement fails and therefore risk.

The prime role of the central clearing counterparty is risk management. The clearing house achieves this objective by using various techniques to manage the exposures taken by its members. The use of margin as a risk management tool requires the member to provide collateral against a deposit requirement designed to protect the clearing house against default caused by a significant movement in the price of an instrument or instruments. This use of margin is made in conjunction with requirements levied on members, which enables the establishing of a default or compensation fund.

CCPs have different structures but in general terms they have the same objectives. The LCH can be used as an example of the kind of structure that we find in a CCP (Figure 2.2).

Settlement of securities involves not just the clearing house but the local and international central securities depositories and the settlement agents of various participants. Their role is to provide a mechanism to hold securities and to effect transfer between accounts by book entry. The main objective is to centralize securities in either immobilized or dematerialized form that will then permit the book entry transfer function to operate for the settlement of transactions.

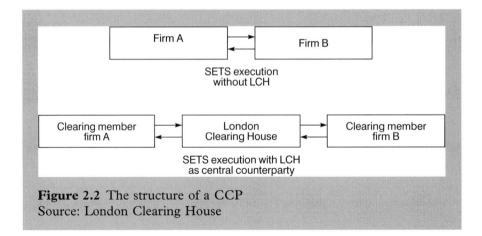

Figure 2.2 The structure of a CCP
Source: London Clearing House

The CSD in a country is known as a domestic CSD and they will often have links with other CSDs to allow streamlined access to cross-border settlement and custody facilities.

There are also international CSDs (ICSDs) and again local or domestic CSDs will link with the ICSDs and vice versa. ICSDs are organizations, of which Euroclear and Clearstream are examples, that started life as settlement and depository service providers for internationally traded bonds. Today that role has expanded significantly and Table 2.1 summarizes the differences between the ICSDs and the CSDs

Table 2.1 Differences between ICSDs and CSDs

ICSDs	CSDs
International client base	Local client base
All securities	Local securities
Settlement	Settlement
Custody	Some additional services
Collateral management	Stock lending
Treasury and other services	Cover domestic activity
Securities lending	
Cover cross-border activity	

There have been many changes, not only in terms of the services and the role of CSDs, but also in the way in which links and alliances have taken place. Clearing, custody and securities depositories are becoming less distinct from each other. Clearstream is a prime example of the new thinking and strategy. As one of the original ICSDs, then called Cedel Bank, Clearstream is today linked to Deutsche Börse, Eurex the derivatives exchange and the clearing houses of the markets. This so-called vertical silo brings together market, clearing and depository including a wide range of custody services.

Euroclear meanwhile is linked to the Euronext market and its clearer Clearnet and has recently joined with SICOVAM, the French depository (Figure 2.3).

The roles of clearing, depositories and custodians is, as we have stressed, changing. What happens to organizations like CREST, LCH and the other thirty or so CSDs in Europe remains to be seen, but the likelihood is that more rationalization will occur, not least because the markets they serve are also being rationalized.

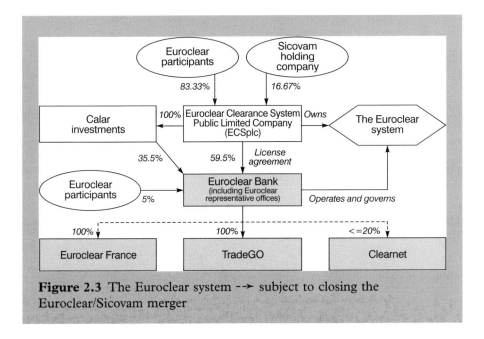

Figure 2.3 The Euroclear system --→ subject to closing the Euroclear/Sicovam merger

Chapter 3

Bond settlement

Introduction

A debt instrument represents a loan from the investor to the issuer and must in most cases be paid back to the investor. The debt instrument will either pay the investor interest at a fixed (hence the term fixed income) or floating rate. In some cases the instrument will instead of paying interest be issued at a discounted price, for example a zero-coupon bond.

There is a wide variety of debt types (i.e. bond, loan stock) each with its own unique features and settlement conventions. However, the bond markets can be divided into two distinct groups, namely international bonds and domestic bonds. The operations team need to be aware of the characteristics of the instruments and their settlement convention.

International bonds

International bond issues are debt securities sold largely outside the country of residence of the borrower. This group may be sub-divided into Eurobonds, now often referred to as international bonds to avoid confusion with the Euro currency and foreign bonds. From an investor's point of view, the differences between a Eurobond and a foreign bond are largely technical. The main differences relate to the

Table 3.1 The differences between Eurobonds and foreign bonds

Eurobonds or international bonds	Bonds are underwritten by an international syndicate of commercial and investment banks.
	Bonds are sold principally in countries other than the country of the currency in which they are denominated.
Example	An issuer with non-USA domicile wishes to raise US dollars outside the USA. The issue is underwritten by international syndicate and initially distributed and subsequently sold outside the USA.
Foreign bonds	Bonds are underwritten by a syndicate composed of commercial and investment banks from one country. ■ Denominated in that country's currency. ■ Sold principally in that country.
Example	An issuer domiciled in a foreign (non-USA) country wishes to raise US dollars in the USA. The issue is underwritten by a syndicate of American banks and initially distributed and subsequently sold in the USA.

composition of the underwriting syndicates and the selling features as Table 3.1 shows.

Foreign bond markets exist in several currencies and are given colloquial names as shown in Table 3.2.

Domestic bonds

Domestic bonds are issued by borrowers resident in the country of issue, denominated in their local currency and regulated by the local authorities. Some of the largest borrowers in the domestic markets are the governments and government agencies plus, to a lesser extent, corporate entities (Table 3.3).

Table 3.2 Colloquial names of foreign bond markets

Name	Currency of issue	Borrower	Market
Yankee bond	US dollars	Non-US	USA
Bulldog bond	Sterling	Non-UK	UK
Matador bond	Euros	Non-Spanish	Spain
Samurai bond	Yen	Non-Japanese via a public issue	Japan
Shibosai bond	Yen	Non-Japanese via a private placement	Japan
Daimyo bond	Yen	As a Samurai, except that they are held in book entry form by Clearstream and Euroclear	Japan

There are two bond types which combine the attributes of International and Eurobond issues:

1 **Global bonds** International bonds placed in both the Euro-markets and domestic markets at the same time and are freely tradeable in any of the major capital market centres. As the issuance of both dollar- and non-dollar-denominated global bonds is rapidly increasing, there might well be less of a distinction in future between a Eurobond and a domestic bond.
2 **Parallel bonds** A parallel bond is a multinational issue consisting of several loans sold simultaneously among various countries each of which raises the loan in its own currency.

There are particular features of bonds that we need to understand as these features determine some of the settlement processes. The features of bonds can be identified by looking at the properties associated with interest payments and maturity requirements of the individual classes of bond.

Table 3.3 Comparison of domestic and international bonds

Characteristics	Domestic	Foreign	International bonds
Issued by	Local borrower	Foreign borrower	Foreign borrower
Domicile of issue	Local market	Local market	International Euro-markets
Issue led by	Syndicate of domestic banks	Syndicate of domestic banks	Syndicate of foreign banks
Denominated in	Local currency	Local currency	Any foreign currency
Regulated by	Securities laws of local country	Securities laws of local country	Not subject to the laws of any particular country

Interest payments are a significant feature and will vary from instrument to instrument. Interest, also known as 'coupon' after the fact that as predominantly bearer instruments, and therefore unregistered securities, the only means of the holder claiming the interest was to detach a coupon from the bond and present it to the issuer. The coupon of interest is payable by the issuer of a bond or loan stock to the holder. The rate of interest refers to the nominal amount rather than the market value of the bond.

Fixed-rate bonds

Fixed-rate bonds pay interest once a year at the same rate of interest for the total life of the bond. Although most fixed-rate Eurobonds and convertible bonds pay interest once a year, there are some foreign bonds, such as US Treasury bonds, which pay twice a year.

Interest on convertible bonds is paid annually while the bond remains unconverted. Usually, once the bondholder elects to convert the bond into equity, the interest payments cease with effect from the date of the last interest payment and any accrued interest will usually be forfeited.

Fixed-income bonds offer investors a guaranteed rate of annual income and the assurance that they will receive the same amount every year until maturity of the bonds themselves. From an operations point of view the interest amount, payment convention and dates and the maturity dates are vital information and need to be held on the database.

Floating-rate notes (FRNs)

This type of instrument has an interest rate that is linked to a benchmark rate and is therefore not a fixed amount during the life of the instrument. Interest on FRNs is usually payable twice a year and occasionally four times a year. The interest rate is changed periodically to match the timing of the interest payments and is usually based on a margin over a pre-specified money market deposit rate such as those illustrated in Table 3.4.

These rates are determined by the major banks independently of each other at 11 am London time every business day.

The interest rate on a FRN is fixed in the following way:

- The paying agent for the issuer takes the LIBOR rates that had been determined by an agreed number of banks (often four) who had previously been nominated as reference banks at the time the FRN was first issued.
- The paying agent fixes the next FRN coupon rate by taking the average of the four reference banks' LIBOR rates and adding the margin.

Table 3.4 Money market deposit rates

Interest rate name	Description
London Interbank Offered Rate (LIBOR)	The rate at which banks offer funds in the interbank money markets. This rate is the usual basis for FRN interest rate calculations.
London Interbank Bid Rate (LIBID)	The rate at which banks pay on deposits in the interbank money market.
London Interbank Mean Rate (LIMEAN)	The average of LIBOR and LIBID.

Example

XYZ issues FRN maturing in 2003. The interest will be fixed quarterly at LIBOR plus 25 basis points and the next fixing is due 30 September.

Reference bank	3-month LIBOR quoted at
Bank A	$5\frac{31}{32}\%$
Bank B	$5\frac{15}{16}\%$
Bank C	$5\frac{15}{16}\%$
Bank D	$5\frac{29}{32}\%$
Average rate	$5\frac{15}{16}\%$
Margin	25 basis points

The interest rate is determined as being $6\frac{3}{16}\%$ (the average reference banks' rate of $5\frac{15}{16}\%$ plus the margin of 25 b.p.) from 30 September to 30 December.

There are variations to this, for instance FRNs issued in Euros would use the Euribor (European Interbank Offered Rate) as the benchmark. Other types of FRN include:

- **Drop-lock FRN** The rate of interest will fluctuate until such time as the deposit rate is at or below a pre-determined rate on an interest fixing date (or sometimes on two consecutive fixing dates). Once this 'trigger' rate has been reached, the interest converts to a specified fixed interest rate for the remaining life of the bond.
- **Mismatch FRN** With mismatched FRNs the interest rate is refixed on a more frequent basis than the interest is paid. The rate will still be based on the six- (or three) month deposit rate linked to the payment frequency.

Example

XYZ issues FRN due 2010 with a nominal amount US$100 000. The interest is fixed monthly at six-month LIBOR plus 25 basis points next six-monthly coupon period from 3 October to 3 April.

From	To	No. days	Coupon rate	Coupon
3 October	3 November	31	$5\frac{1}{4}\%$	452.08
3 November	3 December	30	$5\frac{3}{4}\%$	479.17
3 December	3 January	31	$5\frac{1}{2}\%$	473.61
3 January	3 February	31	$5\frac{3}{4}\%$	495.14
3 February	3 March	28	6%	466.67
3 March	3 April	31	$6\frac{1}{4}\%$	538.19
	Total	182		2904.86

The average rate for the period amounts to approximately 5.75%.

Other FRNS are:

- **Mini-Max FRN** a FRN with a minimum and a maximum interest rate.
- **Capped FRN** a FRN with a maximum interest rate.

- **Flip-flop FRN** relates to the option of the bondholder to convert a FRN with a long maturity date or a perpetual (no redemption date) issue into a FRN with a short maturity date. The bondholder may convert back into the original issue before maturity of the short-dated issue. Although the short-dated FRN will pay a lower margin over LIBOR than the long-dated FRN, the bondholder will receive a capital repayment that much sooner.
- **Convertible rate FRN** a FRN that gives issuers and investors the option to convert from a floating rate of interest to a fixed rate or vice versa and in so doing, allowing them to hedge or speculate against future interest rate movements.

Zero coupon bonds

Zero coupon bonds do not pay interest; they are, however, issued at a deep discount to the par value of the bond and redeemed at the par value. The difference, or capital gain, reflects an effective yield on the bond and might even be taxed as 'income' rather than 'capital'.

Maturity

We can see that there are different ways in which the interest on a bond, loan or note is calculated and paid. As well as the characteristics associated with the interest amounts we need to also focus on the maturity characteristics.

Although bond maturities mostly vary between 3 and 25 years, there are some bonds that will not mature, the perpetual bonds. The maturity terms are set out in the original prospectus document and are broadly divided into three categories. We can look at each in detail starting with normal maturity characteristics.

Bonds are either repayable in one amount on the final maturity date (bullet bonds) or in stages during the life of the bond. These early redemptions may be either mandatory, conditional per the terms stated in the prospectus, or optional.

Mandatory   (Sinking fund)
The issuer redeems a specified amount within pre-set time limits.
If the bonds are trading below par the issuer will usually buy the bonds in the secondary market.
Otherwise the bonds will be drawn by lot and repaid.
Bondholders are informed through advertisements in the financial press.

Example   ABC issues a 7-year bond with a sinking fund.
Year 3 – purchases 10% of the issue
Year 4 – purchases 10% of the issue
Year 5 – purchases 20% of the issue
Year 6 – purchases 20% of the issue
Year 7 – purchases remaining balance (40%) of the issue

Conditional   (Purchase fund)
The issuer will only buy up to a specified amount of bonds if the price of the bonds drops below a certain level in any particular year.

Example   ABC issues a bond with a purchase fund.
Terms of purchase fund – issuer purchases bonds at par if market price drops below 95 during 12 months before final maturity.

Optional   The exact terms and conditions under which bonds may be redeemed will be stated in the prospectus. The decision to redeem bonds early can be either the issuer's or holder's choice.

(Callable bonds)

At the issuer's option the bonds may be redeemed before the final maturity date.

(Puttable bonds)

At the bondholder's option the bonds may be redeemed before the final maturity date.

As we noted above, there are several bonds that do not have a redemption date at all. These are referred to as perpetual or undated bonds.

Example

During the Second World War the British Government issued a $3\frac{1}{2}$% War Loan with an original maturity date in 1952. The government later decided to delay repayment until some later undecided date. With interest rates unlikely to drop below this rate, the outstanding loan of £1.9 billion represents cheap funding for the government.

We have seen how interest and maturity characteristics can be different for each type of instrument and that these characteristics help to determine the settlement process.

We should also consider how bonds are issued and the timetable

New bonds are issued in the *primary market*. It is here that various market participants undertake all the preliminary work and the roles are explained below.

Lead manager

The lead manager, usually a bank, arranges the bond by putting the whole transaction together. This includes:

- Organizing the legal aspects
- Preparing the documentation which varies from country to country and instrument type
- Negotiating the final terms of the bond issue and the timing of the issue with the issuing entity
- Determining the membership of the syndicate of other banks who will be invited to help distribute the bonds
- Allocating and distributing the bonds among the syndicate members

Initially the lead manager will undertake to purchase the entire issue from the borrower. At this moment, the lead manager assumes 100% of the risk associated with the issue. To reduce this risk, the lead manager brings together organizations known as co-leader managers who will undertake to share this risk.

Initial communication with the prospective co-leader managers takes place through a software application known as 'book-runner' which supplies information on computer screens. Thereafter, communication occurs electronically, by fax and sometimes by telex.

Co-lead manager

The issue is allocated to a group of investment banks at the so-called 'fixed price re-offer' (FPRO) level, which is the issue price less a selling concession. The co-lead management group agrees not to trade below the FPRO until the lead manager declares the bonds 'free to trade'. The lead and co-lead managers also receive a combined management and underwriting fee.

This method of issuing bonds, sometimes referred to as a 'bought deal', accounts for 95% of the issuance activity. On occasions, the lead manager will lead an issue on a 'best efforts' basis. Here, the lead manager invites participants into the management group ahead of the issue date. In this scenario, trading might take place in the anticipation of the issue price. This form of trading is known as dealing in the 'grey market'. Newly issued bonds trade in the primary markets anything from one to six weeks after issue.

Market-maker

A market-maker helps to provide liquidity in the market by agreeing to make secondary markets in the bonds. In the UK the market-makers in government bonds are called gilt-edged market-makers (GEMMs).

Trading, whether in the regulated markets or the over-the-counter (OTC) markets has traditionally taken place by telephone. However, today we have electronic bond trading through exchanges like JIWAY and the Cantor Exchange.

Once a trade is executed, both parties to the trade enter into a legally binding obligation or agreement, which commits them to make a delivery of securities from the seller to the buyer in return for the equivalent value in cash. From a settlement point of view there are processes and procedures to be followed.

Trade confirmation

The first task in the pre-settlement phase is to ensure that both counterparties recognize that the details of a particular trade are consistent. This is achieved by the exchange of confirmations that enables one counterparty to allow the other to check all the trade details against its records. As settlement cycles are shortening, counterparties needs to exchange their confirmations more rapidly. The traditional methods of sending paper contract notes and telex transaction confirmations are no longer appropriate and alternative media include electronic trade confirmation (ETC) and SWIFT messages.

It is necessary to perform a prompt confirmation-checking routine so that any problems that arise can be resolved as soon as possible (or within pre-determined deadlines set by the market). Trades that are unconfirmed for whatever reason cannot proceed to the settlement stage.

Instruction

Once the two counterparties have confirmed trade details with each other, the next stage is to pass delivery/receipt instructions to the clearing organization. The task of the clearing organization is to:

- Match delivery instructions with the corresponding receipt instruction, and
- Report the matching results back to the instructing counterparties

Those instructions which are matched are held by the clearing organization until the due settlement date arrives. No further action is required during this period. Obviously problems arising from unmatched instructions must be resolved and correct instructions submitted to the clearing organization for further matching. This stage must be completed in time to meet the clearing organization's processing deadlines. Where electronic markets exist, the confirmation process is automatic.

On settlement day, if there are sufficient assets and cash available for delivery, the trades will settle. The counterparties are advised of their securities and cash movements and, finally, securities ledgers and cash accounting records are updated to reflect these movements.

Settlement, as we noted earlier in the book, is broadly defined as the delivery of an asset in exchange for the equivalent in cash value. Problems of definition arise of 'exchange' when the mechanics are looked at more closely.

There is, for example, a risk of non-receipt of funds if settlement is made by cheque. The cheque takes time to clear and might subsequently be dishonoured by the payer. To reduce this risk, the cash element of settlement should be made in such a way that the cash is both *assured* (i.e. guaranteed) and in *same day funds*.

In addition, settlement of securities and cash should take place at the same time and without the possibility of one party to the transaction countermanding the delivery or payment. Settlement should therefore be the *simultaneous and irrevocable* transfer of ownership of the securities in exchange for the equivalent cash countervalue.

In the bond markets, settlement periods range from T+0 to T+5. Most government bonds tend to settle on T+1 while corporate bonds generally settle on T+3/T +5 cycles.

While there are similarities in the ways in which bonds settle, there are local variations.

International bonds, global bonds and convertible bonds

These bond types are settled by the two clearing houses, Euroclear and Clearstream. Participants of one clearing house can settle trades not only with another participant of the same clearing house but also with participants of the other clearing house. This is known as settlement via the (electronic) bridge which exists between Euroclear and Clearstream.

Through their links to each other (via the bridge) and to external depositories and CSDs, Euroclear and Clearstream are able to accept instructions to settle the following types of transactions:

- **Internal settlements** – these occur between two counterparties who are both participants of the same clearing house.

- **Bridge settlements** – these occur between two counterparties one of whom is a participant of Euroclear and the other a participant of Clearstream.
- **External settlements** – these occur between a local counterparty and a participant of Euroclear or Clearstream across a range of domestic securities.

Cash funding facilities

Euroclear provides secured financing facilities to eligible participants for the purposes of covering securities settlements, pre-advising receipts of funds and, where appropriate, securities borrowing activities. The facilities are secured with cash and/or securities collateral.

Clearstream, for instance, provides financing through an Unconfirmed Funds Facility, a Technical Overdraft Facility or a Tripartite Financing Agreement.

Bond borrowing and lending facilities

Most clearing houses operate borrowing and lending programmes, which include bonds and an increasing number of international equities, in order to facilitate their participants' settlement activities.

Government bonds and domestic bonds

Government and domestic bonds are settled in the local markets but it should be remembered that many of these bond types can also be settled by the International Central Securities Depositories, Euroclear and Clearstream, through their appropriate inter-CSD links.

A key settlement process in respect of all securities is the ability to efficiently fund the settlement. The prime objective is to ensure that there is sufficient cash available to cover all purchases. Inability to pay for securities when presented by the seller for settlement will result in a *failed settlement* and an interest claim from the settlement date up to the date on which the purchase finally does settle. A secondary objective is to make effective use of any cash balances (whether uncommitted or pending trade activities) and in so doing enhance the returns (interest received on credit balances) and reduce the funding costs (on overdrafts and credit facilities).

Cash positioning and cash management is the process that includes cash inflows and outflows from *non-trading events* as shown in Table 3.5.

Table 3.5 Cash inflows and outflows

Cash outflow	Cash inflow
■ Call payments on partly paid bonds	■ Interest receipts
	■ Full/partial redemption proceeds
■ Subscription monies for warrant exercise	■ Receipts of cash to cover anticipated purchases
■ Payments of uncommitted cash balances for money market purposes	
■ Fees, charges, etc.	

Efficient cash management seeks to anticipate future cash movements from a variety of sources in order to ensure that cash is in the right place at the right time, to reduce funding costs and to enhance returns on uncommitted cash balances.

Predicting future cash balances is straightforward when sales, purchases and other events take place as expected. This becomes more problematic when trades fail as it is not usually possible to know the settlement outcome until it has actually taken place. In addition, there will be separate instruction deadlines for transferring sufficient cash to meet the underlying obligation.

In addition to the cash funding, sellers must ensure that there are sufficient securities available for delivery. Where there are insufficient bonds available (through previous failed purchases, turnarounds, short selling, etc.) steps should be taken to deal with this situation. Participants will receive regular reports from their clearing organization or custodian organization listing all the securities and cash balances and will include warnings of any potential or actual restrictions to securities deliveries and cash payments.

However well the pre-settlement processing has gone, there will be settlement failures. Research shows that, on average bond transactions in the developed markets settle on time at a rate in excess of 90%[1]. There are several reasons for settlement failure as shown in Table 3.6.

Table 3.6 Reasons for settlement failure

There are insufficient bonds available for delivery	Selling participant may: ■ Be unable to borrow ■ Be unable to recall bonds out on loan ■ Be awaiting receipt of bonds from purchase
There is insufficient cash	Buying counterparty may: ■ Have cash funding or payment problems ■ Be awaiting proceeds from a sale
Trade instructions are unmatched	■ One or both counterparty(ies) has/have failed to input correct details ■ Both counterparties are in dispute ■ Operational error
Bonds are unavailable for delivery	Clearing organization has blocked deliveries in respect of a corporate event or action.

[1] GSCS Benchmarks – Q3 1997.

The consequences of a failed trade occurring will result in one or more of the following situations:

- One failed settlement might prevent other trades from settling through either lack of securities in sufficient quantity or insufficient cash.
- Funding costs and interest claims will occur.
- Resolving failure problems takes up valuable staff resources.
- Organizations who repeatedly cause trades to fail will get a bad name in the market and counterparties may be less willing to contract business with them.

Therefore resolving failed settlements is important. Depending on the circumstances, the choices are to simply wait until there are sufficient bonds or cash available or alternatively for the seller to try to borrow the bonds. If these options are inappropriate, there are two formal courses of action available:

- **Seller is unable to deliver bonds.** The buyer has the right to issue a 'buy-in' notice to the seller whereby the buyer purchases the bonds from another counterparty ('buy-in' agent) who has sufficient bonds to settle the trade. The original trade is then closed-out and the difference in cash amounts settled between the seller and buyer.
- **Buyer is unable to receive bonds.** The seller has the right to close the trade by means of a 'sell-out'. In this case the seller sells the bonds to another counterparty ('sell-out' agent). The difference in transaction monies plus loss of interest on the sale proceeds is settled between the seller and buyer.

An obvious question is what steps can be taken to reduce the risk of failure?

In bond markets with high volumes, the turnover in a particular issue might exceed the total amount of the issue itself. This could be further impacted if there is a futures contract listed on the derivatives exchange that requires the delivery of a bond in settlement. These situations, allied to the issue being rather illiquid (investors retaining their holdings in custody and not actively trading the issue), might cause a blockage in the settlement chain or simply a shortage of bonds available to deliver.

It might be appropriate for a market to settle trades on a net basis rather than a gross (i.e. trade for trade) basis. Depending on volumes, the options are as follows:

- Trade for trade
- Bilateral netting
- Multilateral netting
- Continuous net settlement
- Real-time gross settlement

How serious is the problem of settlement failure?

The funding costs associated with interest charges and lost opportunities to promptly reinvest cash balances are influenced by the following components:

- The average size (value) of the trade
- Interest rates set in the local market and by the clearing houses etc.
- The proportion of trades that fail to settle on the original settlement date
- The length of time for which they are outstanding

The direct market participants such as the dealers, brokers and market-makers will also be obliged to consider the impact of failed settlements on the organizations' financial resources requirements. The need to bring in further capital to cover this increases the cost, and therefore impacts on the profit and loss of the trade to the organization concerned.

What other settlement issues are there with bonds?

Table 3.7 Types of settlements

Security type	Normal rules
UK government (gilts)	Gilts go 'ex' seven business days before the interest payment date. (An exception is the $3\frac{1}{2}\%$ War Loan which goes 'ex' ten business days before the payment day.)
Eurobonds (held by Euroclear and Clearstream)	Both Euroclear and Clearstream use a record date to establish which bond holders are entitled to receive the interest payment. The record date is usually the close of business, one day before the payment date of the interest. After the record date, settlements are processed ex-coupon.
German bonds	The record date is the close of business, one day before the payment date of the interest.
Netherlands	The record date is the close of business, one day before the payment date of the interest.
Denmark	The record date is one month and one day before the payment date of the interest.
Japan ■ Samurai bonds (bearer) ■ Samurai bonds (reg'd) ■ Daimyo bonds ■ Shogun bonds (bearer) ■ Shogun bonds (reg'd)	Record date prior to interest payment is: ■ 6 business days in Tokyo ■ 21 calendar days ■ 1 business day ■ 1 business day in Tokyo ■ 21 calendar days
Australian global bonds	The record date is 14 days before the payment date of the interest.

Note: Settlement conventions are changing all the time and it is crucially important for operations teams to ensure that they are aware of the current conventions when undertaking settlement.

Custody is a term that relates to a variety of events that take place outside the settlements arena. Once a security has been settled, it must be kept in safekeeping for as long as the investor owns the security. However, further settlements activity might occur as the result of custody-related events including, for instance, the interest payments. Some example conventions are given in Table 3.7.

Once the correct beneficiary has been identified, all that remains is for the interest to be paid. The coupon will be detached from the bond certificate (see Figure 3.1) before being presented to the

Figure 3.1 A bond certificate
Source: The *dsc* Portfolio

issuer's paying agent. The relevant amount of interest, as indicated on the coupon, is paid to the presenter of the coupon (Figure 3.2).

Bond issuers usually make interest payments on either an annual or a semi-annual basis, although there are bonds on which interest is paid quarterly. For fixed-rate bonds, where the amount of interest

Figure 3.2 Coupons
Source: The *dsc* Portfolio

does not change throughout the life of the bond, the amount of interest and the payment date will be printed on the coupon. Interest rates on FRNs fluctuate with movements in the money markets. As the interest rates change, it is not possible to print the amounts on the coupons. For this reason, the FRN coupons will differ slightly from the fixed rate coupons. Issuers advise bond holders of the new interest rate and next payment date by advertising the details in newspapers such as the *Financial Times* and informing the clearing houses, Euroclear and Clearstream, through their depository banks. For holders of Eurobonds held by Euroclear and Clearstream depositories, their cash accounts will be credited on the payment date with same-day value (the exception being Yankee bonds which pay with next-day value).

Should a scenario occur where a trade, dealt 'cum', i.e. entitled to receive the payment, does not settle until after the record date, the coupon is paid to the bondholder who held the bonds on record date, i.e. the seller. With many clearing houses like CREST the system automatically recognizes that the rightful recipient of the coupon should have been the buyer and the result is that the seller's cash account is debited and the buyer's cash account is credited with the full coupon payment. Where bonds settle outside these clearing houses and CSDs, a late settlement will require the claiming of the interest from the seller.

A repayment of capital occurs when there is a partial or full return of the bonds to the issuer in exchange for cash. We have already noted that the terms of any repayments will be included in the original issue prospectus.

There are several instances where this might take place:

- Final redemption
- Early redemption (issuer's call option)
- Early redemption (bondholder's put option)
- Partial redemption (drawing)

The depositories will present the bonds for repayment and debit the participants' securities accounts and credit the cash accounts with value on the repayment date. In order to allow sufficient time to surrender the bonds, the depositories will usually block the positions in order to prevent any further bond movements.

A convertible bond holder is entitled to convert during a conversion period, usually at any time from 90 days after the bond was issued up to the final redemption date. However, any accrued interest is lost on conversion and the price of the bond must allow for the lost interest when calculating the conversion premium.

The bondholder instructs the custodian to withdraw the bonds from custody (from the depository bank) and to deliver them to the conversion agent. The conversion agent will execute the conversion in accordance with the terms of the issue and local market practice. The shares that have resulted from the conversion are subsequently delivered in accordance with the bondholder's original conversion instructions. Furthermore, there will be a delay of several days or weeks before the shares are made available to the shareholder or custodian.

Another corporate action to consider is where a bond has a warrant attached. There are bonds that are issued 'cum-warrant'. These warrants can be split away from the host bond and be exercised at the holder's option into a specified amount of shares at a pre-determined price and at a set time(s) in the future. This 'purchase' or exercise requires the payment of cash to the issuer of the warrant. The subscription terms of the warrant issue will state the exercise price and the date or period during which the exercise might take place. An exercise may take place at a time pre-specified by the issuer. These are either:

- On an annual date; or
- During a pre-defined period; or
- At any time

In terms of giving instructions to exercise their warrant, the holders do much the same as with conversions except that an additional amount of cash must be paid to the issuer in exchange for the underlying shares.

A further key element of the settlement process for securities including bonds is the reconciliation of cash and bond positions.

There are many different situations when bonds are received and delivered and cash is paid and received. These can happen together (delivery versus payment transactions) or separately (conversion of bonds into equity), partially or in full.

Whether securities or cash related, market participants will keep accurate records of all movements and positions. An analogy we could use would be the protection systems used on some railways where the driver's skill and experience are the first line of defence in preventing problems and safe operation but should the driver become ill or make a mistake and pass a danger signal, the train protection system activates the brakes to prevent a catastrophe occurring. Like most safety nets, the 'train protection systems' must work correctly for them to be effective.

Reconciliation, then, is the process by which cash and securities ledger positions are agreed to a third-party's records with any differences or imbalances identified, investigated and resolved without delay. Reconciliation staff need to understand the processes and act as risk managers by analysing the records, identifying the problems and resolving them. To do this work effectively they require various product and personnel skills to enable them to deal with some of the following situations.

Cash (or bank) reconciliations are relatively straightforward to process insofar as the bank statement is compared to the ledger and any unreconciled items recorded on an 'outstanding items sheet' or something similar. In a manual process the following basic steps are applied:

1 Compare bank statement to ledger, ticking-off items that match
2 Identify and record bank statement entries that cannot be identified
3 Identify and record ledger items for which there is no bank statement entry
4 Prepare reconciliation sheet
5 Identify operational sections (if possible) who might investigate items

What makes cash reconciliations so problematic is the sheer quantity of items that pass over a client's account especially when the client uses several of the bank's services. To alleviate the problem, the process is as far as possible automated with only exception reports being produced. This saves time and in any front line or 'safety net' scenario time is of the essence.

Reconciliation of bond positions are performed by comparing the investor's ledger records to those of the custodian or ICSD where the bonds are held, or to the actual bonds physically held in, for instance, the vaults of the organization.

As the reconciliation is prepared from a trade date position and the custodian's records reflect the actual (settled) position, there will be differences, which can be made up of:

- Trades pending settlement
- Failed settlements
- Corporate actions
- Securities lending and borrowing positions
- Bond positions blocked for whatever reason by the custodian

Any additional differences that cannot be accounted for will indicate a problem and should be investigated without delay. It may seem a little obvious but the routine of settlement is a discipline that must be adhered to and invoked if risk is to be managed and the following basic steps should be applied:

1 Compare custodian's balance to ledger, ticking-off items that match or by automated reconciliation
2 Identify and record ledger items for which there are no corresponding custodian balances
3 Identify and record custodian items for which there are no ledger records
4 Prepare reconciliation and outstanding queries data for distribution to relevant people
5 Ensure that outstanding items are investigated and resolved immediately

There are also certain regulatory requirements that pertain to settlement of securities covering areas such as:

- Specifying detailed record-keeping requirements
- Reporting trades and positions to regulators and other authorities, for example the central bank

- Requiring routine counts (including obtaining confirmations from external custodians) and reconciliation with the records of customer investments held
- Client reporting and valuation processes

As part of the comprehensive reporting services provided by the custodians in general and the ICSDs in particular, there will be reports covering most of the operations team's requirements and these are supplemented by reports generated from internal systems.

When we look at the settlement of securities in general and bonds in particular we can see that there are fundamental procedures and processes that make up the bulk of the work. Today much of this is either automated or will become so soon as settlement cycles shorten and electronic trading, clearing and settlement occurs. The settlement of equities is a little different, not least because the settlement conventions are currently longer and most equities are registered not bearer. In the next chapter we look at equity settlement and it is important to note the differences.

Chapter 4

Equity clearing and settlement

Introduction

When an investor purchases a share in a company they have acquired a stake in the equity of that company. Through the share purchase they are buying partial ownership in the issuing company. The number of shares owned by the investor in proportion to the total number of shares outstanding determines the extent of the ownership an investor has in a company. For the private investor this is likely to be a very small percentage, but the larger funds can often have reasonably significant holdings. Not all equity-related instruments give the buyer ownership and it is very important to understand not only the equity shares characteristics but also those of the various other types of instruments.

A share may offer the following 'rights' to investors:

- The **right to vote** in company matters.
- The **right to have access to company books and records** (accounting and record keeping).
- The **pre-emptive right (or right of first refusal)**. This means that if the company issues new securities, the current holders may have the right to purchase additional shares to maintain their proportional ownership of the company. This offer to the original holder is generally given before the offer is made to the public.
- The **right to share in the company's profits** through dividend payments.

These basic rights are important in terms of settlement as they will have actions associated with them, for instance corporate actions in respect of rights issues, dividends, etc. Within the realm of equity securities are various classes of equity instruments such as ordinary shares, preference shares, etc. Foreign markets will support equities, which may be similar to some of the above but with different terminology. For example:

USA – Common Stock/Preferred Stock
France – Action Ordinaire (Ordinary Share)
Germany – Stamm-Aktie (Ordinary Share)
Japan – Futsu Kabushiki (Ordinary Share)

We need to consider the different characteristics of each of the classes of equity instruments, starting with the most common type, the ordinary share, as shown in Table 4.1.

Issuing and trading equities

When a corporate entity offers its shares to the public for the first time, it is said to be going public. This 'Offer for Sale' (or Initial Public Offering – IPO) will be underwritten by investment banks or brokers. A prospectus containing information on the issuer, the terms of the issue, the management structure and any other important aspects of the issuer is prepared. The issue itself will either be placed among clients of the brokers (institutional investors) or advertised to the general public through the publication of mini-prospectuses and application forms in the financial press and elsewhere.

Any shares which are not bought by the public will be taken up by the underwriters who will take the shares onto their own books or sell them on to their own clients. On the other hand, issues that are initially oversubscribed will be distributed on a scaled-down basis. One of the consequences of an oversubscription is that the share price will rise to a premium over the issue price when it starts trading in the secondary market.

Table 4.1 Classes of equities

Class	Characteristics
Ordinary shares	Ordinary shares represent partial ownership in a corporation. Characteristically shareholders will have the right to vote in the election of the board of directors. They will also have the pre-emptive right to purchase any additional shares sold by the company and to receive a dividend, but only if the directors decide to issue a dividend.
	This dividend payment will generally be received when a dividend is declared but only after preferred shareholders have been paid.
	In addition, if the company is liquidated, (un)secured creditors, bondholders, and preferred shareholders have a prior claim to the company's assets before the common shareholders.
Preference shares	Preference shares also represent ownership in a corporation. Characteristically shareholders will:
	■ Generally have no voting rights.
	■ Generally receive dividends before the ordinary shareholders.
	The dividend is frequently fixed as a percentage of the share's stated value. However, **the dividend is not guaranteed**. If the company does not post strong earnings, the directors can omit the preferred dividend.
	A **cumulative** feature may be attached to a preference share, which states that all dividends in arrears must be paid to holders at some point in time prior to any dividends paid to common shareholders.
	Participating preference shares may benefit from an increased level of dividends if the company does well.
	Redeemable preference shares have a fixed repayment date and may be entitled to more than their nominal capital amount (face value).

Table 4.1 Continued

Class	Characteristics
	Preference shareholders generally have priority over ordinary shareholders to the company's assets in the event of bankruptcy or liquidation. Some preference issues have: ■ A **'callable'** feature which stipulates that the issuer may, at a time or times as is in the provisions of the issue, call an issue for redemption. ■ A **convertible** feature making the shares 'convertible' to ordinary shares at maturity or sometimes during the life of the issue.
'A' or non-voting shares	There are some companies that issue shares with restricted or no voting rights. These shares are entitled to receive dividends and, in the event of a liquidation of the company, they rank alongside the ordinary shareholders. Historically families have retained control of the company by holding a majority of voting shares and making the non-voting shares available to the public.
Deferred shares	Deferred shares usually do not qualify for a dividend until the company's profits have reached a pre-set level, or until a particular date.
Designated and foreign registered shares	Shares are sometimes designated for domestic investors and foreign investors and also they can be designated as registered in a particular country. Often these shares are not fungible so, for instance, a purchase of London registered and a sale of Hong Kong registered shares are in fact transactions in two quite separate stocks.

Settlement

Transactions in shares are processed in much the same way as with debt instruments, i.e. trade confirmation followed by instruction matching and final settlement. There are, however, some differences in terms of both methodology and performance.

Shares are becoming increasingly immobilized or dematerialized. This enables shares to be delivered by book entry rather than by physical transfer. In turn this does lead to more efficient settlement but falls short of the overall settlement performance figures of debt instruments. Settlement of many equities is on a T+3 basis in line with the recommendations of G30/ISSA and, as we know, the aim is to reduce this still further to T+1. As settlement cycles shorten, the role of the clearing houses and securities depositories becomes crucial.

As with debt market instruments, equities transactions will also be settled and held through third-party organizations. In some markets, the clearing house will be independent of the depository or one and the same. Historically most third-party clearing houses and depositories have usually dealt with either equities and equity-related instruments or debt and debt-related instruments. In some instances, a single organization, such as the Danish Vaerdipapircentralen, handled a cross-section including bonds, shares, warrants, convertible bonds and unit trust shares. Today, however, as change in the industry leads towards rationalization and centralization in the markets, these organizations are increasingly dealing with multiple products.

In the UK CREST and the LCH provide settlement of equities traded on SETS on a T+3 basis through a central clearing counterparty facility (Equity Clear). CREST also settles bonds, money market instruments via the CMO, unit trusts and open-ended investment companies (OEICs).

The CCP facility is a similar arrangement to that used for exchange traded derivatives and is also in use on Euronext, the combined Belgian, Dutch and French securities and derivatives markets, through the clearing house Clearnet. The international CSDs Euroclear and Clearstream both offer a service based on a variety of securities and funds.

We referred to funding and cash management in the previous chapter. With the comparatively poorer settlement performance of equity transactions, albeit an improving situation, and the issues surrounding registration timing, the funding of equities transactions will be more difficult to manage for the operations team. Consequently, it is likely there will be higher costs associated with this settlement activity and particularly so if we are talking about cross-border settlement.

Settlement fails have just as great an impact on equities as they do on bond settlement. Although clearing houses and custodians offer stock lending and borrowing services, often automatically utilized, to prevent settlement fails and despite the longer settlement cycle, they still occur. A major problem is encountered when a settlement fail coincides with a corporate action. So what kinds of corporate action happen on equities?

Corporate actions

There are various types of corporate action:

- A **benefit distribution** is a distribution made by a company to its shareholders in the form of cash, securities or a combination of both in cases where an entitlement is a fraction of a share. Distributions are usually made in proportion to the investor's holding as at the record date.
- **Cash benefits** include dividends, thus issuing companies will pay a cash benefit, a dividend, to shareholders on a regular basis. This

is typically on a semi-annual or quarterly basis. As the dividends are paid from profits, the amount of cash paid will change from payment to payment and, depending on performance, may not be paid or passed as nonpayment is sometimes called.

As the majority of equities are represented in registered form, it is theoretically straightforward for the issuing company to identify the beneficiaries. Where equities are in bearer form, the issuer will require some form of proof before making a payment. This proof, as with bearer bonds, is in the form of a coupon (or talon), which is detached from the share certificate and presented to collect the amount due.

A problem arises for a 'cum-dividend' purchaser, whose name is not recorded on the company's share register in time to receive the dividend. In order to establish correct entitlement, it is important to understand how some key dates come into play. These dates are the **record date**, the **pay date** and the **ex-date** or **ex-dividend date**.

Record date

The record date is the date upon which the corporation (issuer) or its agent (the Registrar) closes its books for the purpose of capturing the names of the legal owners to whom the distribution will be paid. All legal owners will participate in the distribution, whether or not they are the beneficial owners. In other words, the issuer will pay the 'registered holder'. If shares are sold or given to someone else, they will need to be reregistered in the new owner's name. Until such time as reregistration is performed, the seller is still the legal owner and therefore the initial recipient of any benefits.

As securities are traded, the buyer (the new beneficial owner), or their fiduciary agent (broker, bank custodian), should submit the physical shares to the Registrar (or transfer agent), appointed by the issuing corporation to handle such transactions. The Registrar will cancel the old certificate(s) and issue new ones. The new beneficial owner (or its nominee) has now become the new legal owner. A list of owners will be supplied to the issuer's paying agent in order that they may disburse income payments to shareholders of record on the pay date.

It is not difficult to differentiate the likely problems between certificated and dematerialized equities. On the one hand, there could be long delays in getting the paperwork completed so registration before the record date may not be possible while, on the other, the book-entry process for dematerialized settlement makes it more likely that the registration change will have occurred by the record date. We look further at the issues surrounding dividend payments later in the book.

Pay date

The pay date is the date on which the issuer or the agent pays the distribution to the owners on the record. An important goal is to disburse income payments to clients on time; that is, on pay date. The paying agent may be a financial institution or company treasurer who is named as the organization or person responsible for disbursing payments to share/bond holders on behalf of the issuer.

Ex-date

The ex-date (or ex-dividend date) is the date upon which the security begins to trade without the declared benefit (dividend, interest, etc.). Investors who purchase securities 'cum the entitlement' are entitled to receive any benefits that the issuer decides to distribute. In theory, it is quite possible for a reregistration on such a purchase to be late. In this case the seller would receive the benefit, albeit not being entitled to receive it, and would need to pass on the benefit to the rightful owner.

The local stock exchange will determine a date, known as an ex-dividend date, after which any purchaser will buy without entitlement to the particular current benefit. Instead the seller retains the benefit. This ensures that there should, in the majority of cases, be no need to initiate a benefit claim as the 'cum' transaction should have settled before the record date and any transaction after the 'ex' date but before the record date will not be entitled to this payment.

Repayment of capital

A *capital repayment* is a partial repayment of a company's issued capital. The company pays each shareholder a proportion of the value of the shares at the current market price. While the number of shares issued remains the same, the nominal value of each share is reduced by the amount of the capital repayment per share.

Stock benefits

Some corporate actions are based on stock rather than cash payments. An example of one such action is a rights issue.

Rights issues

A *rights issue* is a further issue of shares offered by a company to its existing shareholders and in proportion to their existing share-holdings as at a record date. Shareholders are offered the right to subscribe for new shares on or before a pre-determined date in a ratio to their holdings at a price below the current market price.

The operations team's first task is to ascertain what the terms of the rights issue are. This will be announced by the exchange and the company and the custodians will provide their clients who have a shareholding with full details of the issue including dates and payment amounts.

There are several options available to a shareholder when a rights issue is announced. The nil-paid rights can be sold for cash, the rights can be accepted and paid for by making a cash payment (known as a call payment) and the nil-paid rights can be allowed to lapse, i.e. neither traded nor accepted. Alternatively sufficient rights can be sold and, with the proceeds, the remaining rights taken up for no cost.

Capitalization

Usually referred to as a *bonus issue*, a capitalization is the free issue of shares to existing shareholders in proportion to the shareholders' balances as at record date. In this case, the shareholder does not need to give any instructions; however, they should be aware of the issue by being informed by their broker or custodian or from company announcements. This is important because the number of shares held will change and so will the price of the shares.

For example, a one-for-one bonus issue is announced with the shares currently priced at £20. An investor currently holds 100 shares. After the bonus issue the investor will have 200 shares and the price will now be £10.

Scrip dividends

Scrip dividends are a method companies use to distribute profits in the form of shares instead of cash. The shareholder is offered the basic benefit of receiving cash or given the option to receive shares. Entitlement to scrip dividends is based on shareholdings on the register as at record date. The number of shares offered takes into account the amount of dividend payable and the underlying market price of the shares.

The operations team and or the custodian must ensure that the dealer's or client's instructions are obtained and passed on. Although the company will usually pay the cash dividend in the absence of any instructions to the contrary, it is important to check the terms of the issue in case the basic offer is for scrip. In most cases, it is possible to issue standing instructions for future scrip dividends.

Stock situations

A stock situation is any event that changes the nature or description of a company's securities. Stock situations are either optional, where the shareholder has a choice, or non-optional, where the shareholder is required to accept the company's decision for the change.

There is the problem of collating sufficient information to allow the dealer or client to make a decision where appropriate and ensuring that the results of the stock situation are correctly received. Examples of *optional* and *non-optional* stock situations are given below.

Take-overs

This is a situation in which a bidding company wishes to obtain a controlling interest in a target company. It is optional for the investor to the extent that he or she can accept or decline the offer within the deadline specified by the bidder.

If, in the terms of the offer, the bidder agrees to take over 100% of the company on condition that there is, say, a 75% acceptance level, then the remaining shares are compulsorily acquired, i.e. the situation becomes non-optional for those shareholders who did not accept the offer.

(Warrant) subscriptions

A subscription is optional and gives the holders of warrants the right to 'exercise' the warrant in exchange for equity by making a subscription payment to the issuing company. If they are not exercised by the last possible date, the warrants expire worthless.

Pari passu lines of a security

This is an area that can cause many problems for the operations teams, custodians and investor alike. A company might issue securities that are identical to existing securities already in circulation except that, for a pre-determined period of time, the new securities do not qualify for a particular dividend or are subject to some other type of restriction. Once this period is over, the two lines of securities are merged and become *pari passu*, they rank equal in all respects.

Until the two lines of securities become *pari passu*, they are given separate security codes and, in addition, will trade at different prices. The operations teams, custodians and investors must be aware of these differences and reflect the holdings accurately in the records.

Liquidations

An investor holding shares in a company that goes into liquidation will be in the situation where the security is probably not only worthless but also un-negotiable. The security will be suspended in the relevant stock exchange(s) until such time as the liquidator is able to repay amounts due to the various classes of creditor. Once there is no more cash that can be retrieved for the creditors, the company is wound up and any certificates or book-entry records cancelled.

This process can take years to resolve and it is important to ensure that any information is received, passed to the client if appropriate and that all expected liquidation payments are collected and, where applicable, paid to the client.

Proxy voting

Proxy voting has been defined by the International Securities Services Association as 'the exercise of the voting right(s) of an investor in shares, bonds and similar instruments through a third party, based on a legally valid authorisation and in conformity with the investor's instructions'. Depending on the country in which the 'proxy' is being exercised, the 'third party' can be a bank, or a person designated by the company, or another shareholder.

Proxy voting generally takes place at shareholders' meetings of companies (annual general meetings and extraordinary general meetings) for the purpose of approving or rejecting certain pre-advised resolutions. Incidentally the same principles generally apply to bond holders' meetings (e.g. in the case of bond issues that are in default and voting about restructuring measures), in which case a special creditors' representative may publicly offer to represent bondholders.

Proxy voting can be subject to more or less stringent restrictions depending on national legislation and company by-laws. In each case, therefore, the legal aspects must be carefully examined. It is also worth noting that in some countries, for instance the United States, voting on company matters is actively encouraged.

In this chapter and in the previous one we have looked at some of the issues surrounding settlement of bonds and equities. Obviously corporate actions are mainly unpredictable and usually have specific deadlines and timings. The settlement process itself is becoming far more uniform with immobilized and dematerialized settlement by book-entry replacing certificates and bits of paper. Also the participants, such as depositories and clearing houses are becoming multi-product based and offer a wide ranging package of services. As T+1 becomes standard so the central clearing counterparty process will become standard and most of the problems associated with settlement will cease to exist.

Until that time the problems of settlement fails and claiming of benefits will occupy the operations teams and managers. In the next chapter we look at the settlement of derivatives and this will enable us to see what the future holds for securities settlement as the CCP is introduced to most of the major equity markets.

Chapter 5

Derivatives clearing and settlement

The development of futures and options

Today, futures and options markets are global and trade contracts on a wide range of products encompassing currencies, commodities, interest rates, shares, indices and even wine and catastrophe insurance. This vast array of products traded today would seem unbelievable to the farmers and merchants of the Midwest of the United States of America who first started trading futures contracts, in a form similar to today, in the mid-1800s. The development of futures markets can in fact be traced back to the Middle Ages and revolved around the supply and demand of farmers and merchants. The early contracts were for delivery of grains such as oats, corn and wheat.

The first futures market

The Chicago Board of Trade (CBOT) was established in 1848 to standardize the size, quality, and delivery date of these commodity agreements into a contract. Once established, the standardization enabled contracts to be readily traded. Thus the forerunner of today's markets was born and farmers or merchants who wanted to hedge against price fluctuations, caused by poor or, for that matter, bumper harvests when, of course, prices would fall, bought and sold contracts with traders or market-makers who were willing to make a different price for buying and selling. Speculators who wanted to gamble on the price going up or down without actually buying or selling the physical grain themselves were also attracted to the market. Therefore liquidity in the contracts was created. Traders were able, if they wanted, to lay off the risk they had assumed from buying and selling with the hedgers by doing the opposite buying and selling with the speculators. The traders' profit was the difference between buying and selling the contracts.

In essence, today's markets do the same job but in thousands of different products. The CBOT, for instance, trades a wide range of contracts on commodities such as soybeans and silver as well as on financial products like Treasury bonds and notes.

In 1874, following in CBOT's footsteps, the Chicago Produce Exchange provided the market for perishable agricultural products such as butter and eggs. After some upheaval in 1898, certain traders broke away and formed what is now known as the Chicago Mercantile Exchange (CME). In 1919 the CME was recognized to allow futures trading. Futures on a variety of commodities have since come to the exchange, including pork bellies, hogs and cattle.

The emergence of financial futures and options markets

In 1972 the CME established a division known as the International Monetary Market (IMM). Its purpose was to enable trading in futures contracts based on foreign currencies. In 1982 the CME started trading futures contracts on the S&P 500 Stock Index so that by the 1990s there were hundreds of different contracts on commodities and financial products. The growth in the volume of financial instruments was phenomenal and it is interesting to note the reasons for this.

In the USA, prior to 1975, nearly all contracts traded were agricultural. Volume in these contracts was less than 10 million per year. However by 1994, the figure had risen to almost 700 million contracts. From the end of the Second World War until the early 1970s there was a very stable economic environment in the USA helped by the Bretton Woods Agreement, which kept interest rates in a narrow range. However, when the US dollar was devalued, partly as a consequence of the funding of the Vietnam War and a heavy domestic spending programme, uncertainty and fluctuation in interest rates replaced the economic stability. Europe and Japan had also recovered in economic terms from the rebuilding effects of the Second World War and with their economies growing the dollar came under severe pressure. The need to be able to hedge (or to protect) against the risk associated with volatile currencies and interest rates became critical for many businesses and industries. Therefore we saw the birth of the first financial contracts, which became the corner-stone of the futures and options industry as we know it today.

Therefore, in 1975 the CBOT launched the first futures contract on a financial instrument, the Ginnie Mae Mortgage Bond future, followed by the CME, which listed a Eurodollar contract. Shortly after the CBOT listed what was to become for many years the world's most heavily traded futures contract, the Treasury bond future.

Since then, the growth in volume of futures and options contracts in the USA and the rest of the world has, as we have seen, been phenomenal, as more and more exchanges have opened and a plethora of financial products are listed to meet the demand for risk-hedging mechanisms.

This process continues today as new markets open in the developing countries. However, the emergence of futures and options markets outside of the USA has seen a change in the make-up of the volume of business traded, although the USA still has three of the largest markets in the world. Today Eurex, the combined German and Swiss market, is the largest exchange by volume of contracts traded. The Euro Bund future traded on Eurex is the heaviest traded futures contract in the world and, to illustrate the global nature of today's

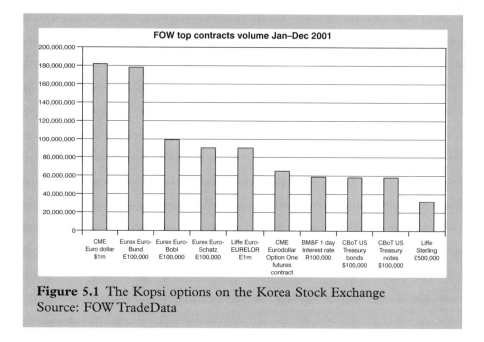

Figure 5.1 The Kopsi options on the Korea Stock Exchange
Source: FOW TradeData

market, the Kopsi options traded on the Korea Stock Exchange was in 2001 the heaviest traded contract in the world (see Figure 5.1).

Mergers and alliances between derivative markets and stock exchanges have been common through the last two years and today we have Euronext, the combined stock and derivative markets of France, Belgium and the Netherlands, the Singapore Exchange (SGX) formed from the merger of the Singapore International Monetary Exchange (SIMEX) and the Stock Exchange of Singapore and the joining of the Hong Stock Exchange and the Hong Kong Futures Exchange. Many others are in the offing.

The first options markets

Like futures, the use of options can be traced back to the eighteenth century, and in certain forms as far back as the Middle Ages. In the eighteenth century options were traded in both Europe and the USA, but unfortunately due to widespread corrupt practices the market had a bad name.

These early forms of option contracts were traded between the buyer and seller and had only two possible outcomes. The option was delivered (i.e. the underlying product changed hands at the agreed price) or it expired without the buyer taking up an 'option' to exercise the contract for delivery. In other words there was no 'trading' of the option positions, and worse, in the early days no guarantee that the seller would honour his or her obligation to deliver the product if the buyer exercised his option.

In April 1973, the CBOT proposed a new exchange, the Chicago Board Options Exchange (CBOE), to trade stock options in a standardized form and on a recognized market where performance of the option contract on exercise was guaranteed. This was the birth of 'traded options'.

Since then option markets have grown in the USA and globally. Like futures markets, they cover a wide range of products, including options on futures. Although options have been trading for a shorter time than futures they are nevertheless extremely popular with both hedgers and speculators alike.

The growth of futures and options continues

Today, as we have already noted, the derivatives industry is truly global. To illustrate just how big the industry is we only need to look at the volume of contracts traded on worldwide derivatives exchanges during 2001, which totalled a staggering 35 billion-plus contracts.

We must also take into account the derivatives business that is not traded on exchanges. In 1999, the market in *over-the-counter* derivatives was estimated by the Bank for International Settlements to be valued at $70 trillion. The industry, both exchange traded and over-the-counter, continues to grow with new exchanges and new products providing users with the medium to control risk.

Recently introduced products include weather derivatives, share futures, flex options and 'mini' (smaller contract size than the standard futures contract) contracts on for instance the FTSE and S & P indices.

To understand the clearing and settlement of derivatives we need to understand the characteristics of the products. So we can ask the questions, what exactly are futures and options? What are swaps and OTC options?

Derivatives

There is a lot of jargon surrounding the futures and options industry and to make matters more confusing there is often more than one word that has the same meaning. The generic term that is used is **derivatives**. It encompasses many different products and means more than just futures and options.

A definition is:

> **A financial instrument whose value is dependent on, or derived from, the value of an underlying asset.**

To break this down into more specific types of products we can define a futures contract as:

> **A *futures contract* is an agreement or legally binding obligation to buy or sell an asset at a certain time in the *future* for a certain price that is agreed today.**

A futures contract is where the buyer enters into an obligation to buy on a specific date and the seller is obliged to sell on a specific date. Exchange-traded futures contracts are standardized in terms of size, quantity, grade and time. Elements of the settlement process will be directly related to the product specification. For instance, futures contracts and options on futures are *marked to market* every day. This is the daily payment of the profit or loss against the previous day's settlement price and is known as *variation margin*. This variation margin is the result of the value of the movement in price as determined by a number of what is called *ticks*. A tick has a monetary value and therefore the variation margin equals the number of ticks multiplied by the value of the tick multiplied by the number of contracts held. Each day this variation margin is called or paid out by the clearing house from or to the member and it must be settled by a specific time.

Example

A sale of 20 LIFFE June Long Gilt Bund futures @ 107.39 can be made as an **opening** position. That evening the closing price determined by the exchange is 107.25.

The contract specification published by the exchange tells us the minimum price movement and tick value is 0.01 and £10.

The variation margin for settlement the next day (T+1) is:

14 ticks (107.39–107.25) × £10 × 20 contracts = £2800

As we have sold the contracts and the price has fallen we have made a profit of £2800.

The seller does not need to have an existing long or bought position. As a result of the above transaction the seller would now have a short position. To remove the obligation they would need to buy an equal number of June futures to close out the position or on expiry of the contract they would go to delivery. We look at this process again later in the chapter.

Forwards are very similar to futures contracts and can be traded on an exchange or over-the-counter. They are often not marked to market daily but settled only on the delivery date or on a pre-determined date during the life of the contract.

Commodity futures

These are slightly different contracts due to the nature of the underlying products. Financial institutions, because of the implications of physical delivery of the actual commodity, do not generally use commodities and commodity derivatives. The exception to this is if they are utilized in retail products like funds and investment trusts. They are mostly used by specialist companies involved with the commodity in some way such as a cocoa exporter and a chocolate manufacturer.

Obviously, agricultural and soft commodities are perishable and have a limited life; therefore the delivery process must be carefully adhered to. Delivery issues include warehousing, transportation and product standardization requirements. Agricultural and soft commodities are finite in terms of availability and there can also be significant differences in terms of the quality of products due to forces of nature such as drought, flood, fire, etc. In order to ensure that the product delivered is of the correct quality as defined in the contract there is a vetting procedure. Where there is a problem with delivery, arbitration would be sought. This may be via a trade association or an independent source appointed by the exchange.

The delivery months of agricultural and soft commodities are not as standardized as other futures contracts. This is because they have to take into account factors such as harvesting, shipments and transportation. During the delivery period the clearing organization may demand higher margins in order to force traders who do not wish to go to delivery to close their positions.

Purchase of 50 LIFFE July Cocoa futures @ 1070

The buyer has entered into an obligation to take delivery of coffee from the holder of a short position in July of the year of expiry. The price is set at £1070 irrespective of the price coffee might be trading at in July. The buyer has locked in the price at £1070.

Options

An *option* is in the case of the **buyer**:

The *right* but not the obligation to take (call) or make (put) delivery of the underlying product

and in the case of the **seller**:

The *obligation* to make or take delivery of the underlying product.

An option contract is either a call or a put as described above. The specifications of an options contract, in addition to the type, include:

- **Expiry date** The last date on which an option holder can exercise their right. After this date an option is deemed to lapse or be *abandoned*.
- **Exercise price** The fixed price, per asset or unit (sometimes called *strike price*) at which an option conveys the right to call (purchase) or put (sell) the underlying asset or units.

- **Premium** The sum of money paid by the buyer, for acquiring the right of the option. It is the sum of money received by the seller for incurring the obligation, having sold the rights, of the option. Premium is paid or received on trade day plus one (T+1).

Other common terms that are associated specifically with options are:

- **In-the-money** A call option where the exercise price is below the underlying asset price or a put option where the exercise price is above the underlying asset price. These options are deemed to have intrinsic value of the in-the-money difference between the exercise price and the underlying asset price.
- **At-the-money** An option, whose exercise price is equal, or closest to, the current market price of the underlying asset. This option has little or no intrinsic value as there is no in-the-money difference between the exercise price and the underlying asset price.
- **Out-of-the-money** A call option whose exercise price is above the current underlying asset price or a put option whose exercise price is below the current underlying asset price. This option has no intrinsic value.

When making an opening purchase the buyer of an option becomes known as a position *holder, buyer* or *taker* and is said to be *long* of the market. When making an opening sale the seller of an option becomes known as a position *writer, seller* or *granter* and is said to be *short* of the market.

Option positions can be either long or short. In special circumstances, both long and short positions can be held *gross*. Long or short option positions are normally closed out at the time of transacting the opposite position.

Sale of 100 LIFFE BT May 600 Calls @ 69

The seller or writer of this option has opened a short position giving the buyer or holder of the option the right to ask for delivery of British Telecom shares at 600 p any time until expiry of the option in May.

For that right the buyer has paid the seller a fee called a premium of 69 p. Each contract is for 1000 shares so the seller has received a premium of £69 000 (100 000 × 69 p) but must deliver the shares at 600 p irrespective of the price of BT in the market if the buyer exercises their right.

Clearly the buyer is expecting the shares to be above 669 p (600 p + 69 p) by May.

In settlement terms there is a difference between futures which have a daily variation margin process and options where the premium related to the buying and selling of the right is settled T +1 and then another transaction occurs if the buyer exercises their right.

Options on futures

Options on futures have the same characteristics as the options described above. The difference is that the underlying product is either a long or short futures contract. A premium is not paid or received as the contracts are marked to market each day.

Example

+ 70 LIFFE Long Gilt June 107.00, Put options @ 1–06

The buyer has bought the right to a short position of 70 futures at 107 (the seller will therefore have to assume a long position) and has paid the seller the premium of 1–06.

In this case on expiry this option would become a short position, because it is a put option, of 70 LIFFE Long Gilt June futures at 107.00.

Exchange characteristics

An exchange or market is where members, who can be corporates or individuals, trade futures and options. They carry out their business under the rules and regulations of the exchange. The exchange in turn is subject to regulation by the domestic government agencies. For example, in the UK, LIFFE is a recognized investment exchange (RIE) under the main regulator the Financial Services Authority (FSA).

Some exchanges are open-outcry which means that the members gather together physically on a market floor in pits and shout their bids and offers. Traders use an exchange-authorized method of hand signals to communicate with their colleagues and other market members. Others are electronic where members enter bids and offers via a screen. This is known as *screen-based* or *electronic trading*.

Some exchanges operate a combination of both systems for all or some of the day in certain contracts.

Exchange membership

The responsibility of the management of exchanges is normally vested in the chief executive or board of directors. They are elected to the board and represent a cross-section of the membership of the exchange. Reporting to the board are their appointed practitioner committees who consider specific issues relevant to the day-to-day operation of the exchange. These issues typically concern floor trading, product development, membership and rules and default and risk management. Each exchange has a membership, which normally is drawn from all parts of the financial services industry. LIFFE's membership originates from many international countries but many exchanges have a mostly domestic membership.

Membership is generally broken down into two categories – non-clearing and clearing:

1 **Non-clearing membership** is for companies who wish to execute business only on the exchange. This is further broken down into companies who execute business only for themselves, also known as *proprietary traders* or *locals*, and companies who execute client business as well as their own.
2 **Clearing members** are companies who execute business, in any capacity, but also clear or settle that business with the exchange or clearing house.

Again this is broken down into two further categories – those companies who only clear their own business and those who clear other non-clearing members business as well as their own.

Many exchanges such as LIFFE, Deutsche Börse and the Chicago Board of Trade have converted from mutual status to having shares and becoming 'for-profit exchanges'.

The role of the clearing house

We looked at the role of the clearing house in Chapter 2 so now let us consider how this impacts specifically on the derivative markets. The role of the clearing house is to act as a counterparty to both sides of the trade thereby breaking the direct counterparty relationship between the two trading counterparties. It is fundamental to the integrity and credibility of the market for which it operates, as its purpose is to guarantee the performance of each and every transaction. By assuming the legal responsibility for the trade, the clearing house removes any risk on each other that the two original counterparties might have had.

There are two main types of clearing house; those that are a division of the exchange itself and indistinguishable from the exchange who owns them, and those that are more independent of the exchange. In most cases, for these independent clearing houses, the members of the markets provide the financial backing.

The London Clearing House (LCH) and the Options Clearing Corporation (OCC) in Chicago are somewhat different from other derivative clearing houses as they clear for more than one exchange. This is advantageous for the broker as clearing members of LIFFE, LME and IPE in London, for example, as it means only one point of settlement for all of their trading in these markets.

Clearing houses must be financially robust in order to sustain a default in the market(s) for which they operate. The financial standing of the clearing house is a very important consideration for brokers when they are contemplating becoming clearing members of an exchange. It is also an important issue for companies researching the potential of trading in the market, as they need to know that their trades will be efficiently settled and that their positions will be secure in the event of another unrelated party causing a default in the market.

As stated above, FSA have designated LCH as a recognized clearing house and regulates the LCH. This gives the members and users of the market comfort that it is a properly organized and approved clearing house.

The process of creating the trade in the name of the clearing house as counterparty to each member is called **novation**. In this process the clearing house becomes buyer to every seller of each transaction and seller to every buyer of each transaction. At this point, the clearing member has no counterparty risk in the market for their trade other than with the clearing house. All open positions are only held with the clearing house and it becomes irrelevant which market member the trader dealt with originally. Once this process is completed, the clearing house is in a position to effect settlement of the two transactions. A simple example of the use of derivatives is given below.

Example

Potato farmers and futures and options
Imagine a potato producer. In March, at the beginning of the season he must purchase the seeds to plant his potato crop and will tend his crop during the coming months until harvest time. He has no idea at that time how the season will turn out but his livelihood depends on the profits that he can make from growing his potatoes. He looks to the futures market to 'hedge' or protect his potato crop.

The farmer has two fields with an estimated yield of 375 tonnes in each field. He has fixed overheads of £5000 to produce the potatoes and expects to sell them at around £10 to £12 per tonne.

In order to protect his crop against a fall in prices and to ensure that his overheads are covered the farmer enters into a futures contract. He sells 25 contracts (20 tonnes per contract = 500 tonnes) at £10 per tonne for delivery in October. This would cover the £5000 fixed costs that he has as he is guaranteed to sell 500 tonnes at £10 per tonne in October. He also has his additional 250 tonnes to sell at the prevailing market price, on which he will make a profit. However, the farmer still has a problem, as what would happen if he were unable to produce the 500 tonnes that he needs to fulfil his contract?

In this case the farmer enters into a hedging transaction to protect himself. He buys a call option, which gives him the right to buy 500 tonnes at £10.50 per tonne in October. To acquire this right costs him £250 in option premium. This is his insurance in case his harvest fails and in total it costs him £500, because he has paid £250 in option premium and it will cost him an extra £0.50 per tonne if he has to exercise his option (500 tonnes × £0.50 per tonne = £250). He would have chosen the £10.50 call option because it was not far from the £10.00 price he wanted and was cheaper to purchase.

At harvest time in October the farmer's crop is poor and potatoes are in short supply. He has managed to produce only 520 tonnes from his crop. However, the market price of potatoes given the shortage is £16 per tonne.

The farmer must fulfil his futures contract obligation by selling 500 tonnes at £10 per tonne but he sells his additional 20 tonnes at £16 per tonne.

Sell 500 tonnes @ £10 per tonne	= £5000 cr.
Sell 20 tonnes @ £16 per tonne	= £320 cr.
Net profit before hedge	£5320 cr.

He also has the option, which he should now exercise because it is in-the-money and allows him to buy 500 tonnes at £10.50 per tonne, which he can resell in the market at £16 per tonne to make a profit.

Buy 500 tonnes @ £10.50 per tonne	= £5250 dr.
Sell at market price of £16 per tonne	= £8000 cr.
Gross profit	= £2750 cr.
Less option premium paid	= £250 dr.
Net profit on hedge	= £2500 cr.

Overall profit on transactions   = £7820 cr.

Let us look at what happened if the crop had been successful and the farmer was able to produce 900 tonnes of potatoes. Because of the good crop and plentiful supply, the market price of potatoes has fallen to £7 per tonne. He fulfils his obligations in the futures market. The option contracts that he bought as insurance for his crop are out-of-the-money and therefore are left to expire worthless.

Sell 500 tonnes at £10 per tonne	= £5000 cr.
Sell remaining 400 tonnes at £7 per tonne	= £2800 cr.
Gross profit before hedge	= £7800 cr.
Option premium paid	= £250 dr.

Net profit   = £7550cr

If the farmer had not entered into any futures or options transactions he would have been able to sell his total crop of 900 tonnes at the market price of £7 per tonne, thus realizing a profit of £6300.

Using the futures and options not only protected his crop but also gave him a better profit than without the protection.

Problems with derivatives

We have all read about the problem that certain companies have had with derivatives trading but you can see from the above example that if used properly they are excellent tools for risk management. The problems that have occurred have been in situations where derivatives have been misused. In some cases there has been speculating when there should have been only hedging transactions taking place. In all cases there has been a clear lack of understanding of the products and the risks that are involved coupled with a lack of controls and monitoring of procedures.

There have been well-publicized 'problems' with derivatives and yet we must never lose sight of the fact that millions of contracts are traded quite safely by numerous organizations around the world. Those contracts are doing the job they were intended to, i.e.

Transferring risk from those that wish to get rid of it to those that wish to assume it.

Part of the clearing and settlement of derivatives is all about managing risk and the role of margin in this process is very significant. Let us look at the margin process in some detail.

Margin

We have already briefly looked at variation margin but we need to look at this again and also at other margin that is applied in derivative settlement.

Initial margin

The deposit which the clearing house calls to cover margin requirements is called *initial margin* and is returnable to the clearing member once the position is closed. The amount for each product will vary as it is geared to the current volatility of the particular product. The margin will be sufficient to cover an approximate 3–5% movement in the price of the contract on a day but can and often is changed to reflect the current situation. If this occurs during the day it is called *intra-day margin*. This will only occur when there is a very large movement up or down in the price of the contract.

When you buy or sell a futures contract you do not pay the full value of the contract, only the margin requirement. This deposit is held by the clearing house throughout the time that the position is maintained. The clearing house must have some kind of insurance that any delivery obligations could be fulfilled. Options on futures positions are margined in the same way as futures contacts with initial and variation margin requirements.

Long premium paid option positions are not charged initial margin because once the premium has been paid for the option, on trade day +1, then there is no further risk to the clearing house. The worst that can happen is that the option can expire at zero. If a long option is exercised then the clearing house will call margin to cover the delivery obligations. Short option positions are margined, as there is a risk of the writer being unable financially to fulfil their delivery obligations. This margin requirement is typically calculated using SPAN (standard portfolio analysis of risk) or a similar exchange margin method such as theoretical inter-market margining system (TIMS) as explained below. It varies from clearing house to clearing house whether interest is paid to members on cash deposited to cover their initial margin requirements. At LCH interest is paid on cash balances using rates which are actually set by the clearing house. These rates are known as the London Deposit Rates (LDR) and they are derived from bid rates for overnight funds quoted by selected money brokers and major banks for each currency. The highest and lowest rates are discounted to calculate the average.

Many brokerage houses use the LDR rates plus 1% or minus $\frac{1}{2}$ as a basis of rates charged or paid to their clients.

An explanation of delta

The delta of an option can be described as the speed with which an option's premium moves, in respect to the changes in the underlying security price. As time value decreases, this also affects the delta of an option. A deep in-the-money option has a delta of 1, a far out-of-the-money option a delta of 0 and an at-the-money option a delta of 0.5.

SPAN, a risk-based margin system (see page 87), uses the delta value of options to convert them to equivalent futures when calculating the inter-month spread charge, because gains in one month may not exactly offset losses in another and there is a risk for the clearing house.

Intra–day margin

As we have already mentioned, in times of very large movements up or down in the price of a contract the clearing house or exchange will recalculate the initial margin requirement. An additional amount may be required per contract for all contracts open which are affected. It is unlikely that all contracts are affected because the news that caused the volatility may concern, for example, a foreign economy, which has a knock-on effect for domestic bonds. If the clearing house believes that the situation is only temporary and that conditions will quickly return to a more stable environment, then they will leave the initial margin requirement at its original level for the next day, only calling the intra-day margin as a one-off payment. More likely, however, the initial margin level will be changed as a result of volatile conditions. The intra-day margin call is made to cover the increased risk since the original initial margin was paid in the morning, and then the new increased initial margin rate is called from the next day onwards.

Intra-day margins can be called from the clearing members by the clearing house up to any time as determined in their rules. The clearing members must pay the required amount to the clearing house. However, depending on the time of day that the call is made, it may be difficult for the clearing member to receive the funds from their clients. They must endeavour to receive the funds and at the very least must contact the client and let them know that additional funds are due. In this respect, it is necessary that the clearing member is able to recalculate margin requirements during the day on their own systems so that they may see accurately which clients are affected and reconcile the amounts that are due.

Spot month margin

This is an additional rate of margin which is charged by the clearing house to cover the risk that they incur between the last trading day of a contract and its ultimate delivery. It covers the risk of a default during the delivery process. There are no offsets allowed for spread positions. The clearing house on settlement day +1 releases initial and spot month margins, once they are satisfied that delivery has been effected correctly.

Margin methods

The method for calculating margin also varies from one clearing house to another. It may be different for futures and traded options. However, in 1988 the CME devised a method known as **SPAN**, which stands for standard portfolio analysis of risk. This risk-based margining system is now used by many exchanges for the calculation of the initial margin on futures and options. Most exchanges that have adopted SPAN have 'tweaked' it for their own particular use and therefore there are different versions in use. For example, LIFFE use London SPAN.

SPAN looks at a set of sixteen possible changes in market conditions within the boundaries of the risk parameters set by the clearing house which is known as the risk array. The profit or loss for one long position in each futures and options contract is worked out under each scenario, for valuing positions. By combining all the individual arrays, London SPAN determines the scanning risk, which is the worst possible loss for the portfolio. Each position in the member's portfolio is calculated and totalled across the same underlying contract. The final result is the largest potential loss for the portfolio, which is charged as initial margin.

London SPAN uses pricing models to calculate the option prices. The Binomial model is used for equity and index options but the Black–76 model is used for options which are priced off the future. The parameters are set using both the historic and implied volatility of the contract, and in agreement with the exchange. A detailed explanation of SPAN is provided in Appendix 2.

Margin offsets

Where investors in a market employ particular trading strategies then the clearing house may allow certain reductions in the margin requirements to reflect the reduced risk of the position. In the US markets, for example, a 'hedge' rate of initial margin is quoted which can be applied to positions that are a hedge. This is a position where the opposite side reduces the risk of one side of the position.

Movements in the market would have a negative impact on one side but a positive impact on the other. This would be a significantly lower initial margin rate than a 'spec' rate, which carries the full risk of the position, as there is no balancing side to offset any of the risk.

London SPAN calculates an inter-month spread charge to compensate for the basis risk incurred because futures prices do not correlate exactly across contract months. This is calculated for futures and using the delta value for options to convert them to equivalent futures. Where a spread exists but does not have equal and opposite sides then spread margin is only charged on the number of contracts that are equal. The remaining contracts are charged margin at the full rate.

The inter-month spread charge calculation is:

Number of spreads × inter-month spread charge rate

Additionally certain different contracts can be offset across portfolios, where the clearing house can justify it on risk grounds.

Delta spreads are used in the calculation:

Weighted futures price risk × spread credit rate × number of spreads × delta spread ratio

In order to calculate the total initial margin requirement, the following rule is applied:

Scanning risk **plus** inter-month spread charge **plus** spot month charge **minus** inter-commodity charge

Variation margin

For most types of futures contracts, the clearing organization pays and collects the profit or loss that is accruing on the open futures positions as the price moves up or down each day. This movement generates pay and receive situations for the members with the open positions. The clearing organization will call in and pay out this net amount to each clearing member daily. This amount is known as variation margin (VM).

For other types of futures contracts, usually known as forwards, the variation margin is calculated each day but any profits accrued are not paid out until the settlement date of the contract. This applies even if the position is closed out in the exchange early on in its life. The profit will stay with the clearing house until the settlement (delivery) date. Any profit that is accrued can be used to offset initial margin requirements but it does not attract interest, as it is unrealized. All losses that occur must be settled on a daily basis.

Example

Another calculation of variation margin
The client buys 1 September Long Gilt Future at 109.13 on 1 June and then sells the position at 109.42 on 8 June.

The contract size is £100 000 nominal value with a minimum price fluctuation of one pence per £100 nominal or 0.01. This gives a tick size of £10.

Date	Trade price	Net position	Closing price	Daily price movement	Sett. date	Daily settlement
1/06	109.13	+1	109.09	−4 ticks	2/06	£40 Loss
2/06		+1	109.28	+ 19 ticks	3/06	£190 Profit
3/06		+1	109.28	No change	4/06	No Movement
4/06		+1	109.35	+ 7 ticks	5/06	£70 Profit
5/06		+1	109.40	+ 5 ticks	8/06	£50 Profit
8/06	109.42	0		+ 2 ticks	9/06	£20 Profit
Total				**+ 29 ticks**		**£290 Profit**

The profit on the trade was 29 ticks or points, which is the difference between the buying and selling price.

Each tick = £10 therefore 29 × £10 = £290

The initial margin of £500 per contract would be called from the clearing house on 13/1 and held until 20/1 when it would be returned.

It must be remembered that variation margin must always be settled in cash. This is because the broker must always settle with the clearing organization in cash as for every profit that is paid out by the clearing house there must be an equal loss being paid into the clearing house. Clients without cash in place to cover variation margin may incur harsh debit interest penalties.

Tick size

The tick size of a contract is not always worked out in the same way.

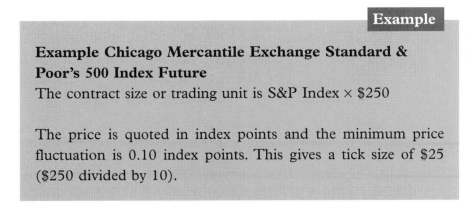

Example

Example Chicago Mercantile Exchange Standard & Poor's 500 Index Future
The contract size or trading unit is S&P Index × $250

The price is quoted in index points and the minimum price fluctuation is 0.10 index points. This gives a tick size of $25 ($250 divided by 10).

Example

LIFFE Short Sterling Interest Rate Contract
The tick size is the value of a one-point movement in the contract price. This price is arrived at by multiplying the notional contract size by the length of time of the notional time deposit underlying the contract in years multiplied by the minimum tick size movement of 0.01%:

£500 000 × 3/12 × 0.01% = £12.50

The tick size of the Short Sterling Future therefore = £12.50

Collateral

Initial margin obligations at the clearing house can be covered in various ways. Collateral in the form of cash in the currencies of the contracts traded is most commonly used. In addition bank guarantees, government treasury bonds and bills, certificates of deposits and certain equities are accepted at the London Clearing House, for example. Each clearing house or exchange will publish the collateral that they accept. LCH has quite a wide range but some markets accept cash only in their domestic currency.

It is possible to use a combination of cash and physical collateral in some markets. For 10-year Japanese Government Bond Futures in the Tokyo Stock Exchange, however, only a maximum of 2% of the margin requirement may be covered using collateral and the remaining 1% must be cash.

The collateral that the broker will accept from a client is usually negotiable. There may, however, be restrictions about where it must be held and also an arrangement fee. In some cases, the client may have to check with their trustees about whether they have any additional restrictions. By physically transferring the collateral into the name of the clearing member or clearing house, the client loses 'beneficial ownership' of the collateral. Therefore, there is a credit risk with the clearing member (or wherever the collateral is held) as it is shown as their assets and may be seized in the event of a default by the organization, even though the client is not involved in the default situation.

Acceptable collateral

Most of the exchange clearing houses publish lists of acceptable collateral. It must be understood that these are lists of collateral accepted from the clearing member. The clearing member may or may not be prepared to accept the same collateral from a client. Even where it does agree, it may levy additional charges to cover the administration costs.

Margining to a client

It is relatively easy to understand the concept of variation margin. It is possible for the client to calculate the amounts themselves in order to verify what their clearing broker is charging or paying them. Depending on the complexity of the position, it would be easily possible for the clients to work it out for themselves using a pen, paper and a calculator, so long as they know the necessary variables such as the tick size and value.

Initial margin is much harder to explain. For futures contracts where an initial margin rate is published by the clearing house, it can be easily calculated and verified by clients, but only if the position is very simple and no offsets have been given under a portfolio margining system. The biggest problem can occur if the client wants to trade a particular strategy and needs to know approximately how much the initial margin will be, so that they can work out the financing costs. It may be possible for some clearing brokers to run test accounts for clients where such positions could be input and the margining run using the last available arrays. This would give the approximate cost but can be very time consuming for the broker's staff to accomplish and would not be part of a regular service to the client.

Although risk-based margining systems are very efficient and result in the client paying a lower overall initial margin, clients can find it very difficult to understand and generally have to accept the clearing broker's word that the amount required is correct. In order for the client to accurately verify the initial margin required, they need to be able to receive the risk arrays from the clearing house or exchange and then have a system which is able to compute this correctly. Some clearing houses publish their risk arrays openly and clients are able to obtain the information easily. However, a charge is usually made for this service. Other exchanges do not openly publish the arrays except to their clearing members. Additional problems occur for clients who have a portfolio of global market positions, so it becomes almost impossible for clients to perform margining themselves.

For larger-volume clients, one solution may be to use a recognized futures system for their own processing and accounting. Systems such as Rolfe & Nolan are available on a bureau basis so clients pay only for the use that they make of the system. These systems should have all the margining capabilities already established.

Single-currency margining and settlement

For clients trading in various different markets around the world and having numerous currencies to move, the settlement process can be quite cumbersome. Therefore, many clearing brokers offer a service known as single-currency margining. If you remember, this is not unlike the service offered by the custodians for securities.

This involves the deposit of one currency which is equal to or more than the total amount of currencies due. In order to calculate this, each currency is notionally converted to the base currency chosen by the client as the preferred settlement currency. Interest would normally be received on the currency deposited and would be charged on the currencies, which are in debit. Both the clearing broker and the client incur an intra-day FX risk, as the amount due in the settlement currency is only calculated once overnight, using the end-of-day FX rates. Therefore, if this service is offered to many clients it needs careful control by operations management to ensure that FX risks are properly managed. Even major currencies need to be monitored so that the management team is aware of exposure to each currency. Additional problems can arise with some of the minor global currencies, as these are not always readily available for use. It may be useful for the clearing broker to have an agreement for single-currency margining, which stipulates those currencies included under normal use and what should happen for the exceptional currencies.

Although no formal charge is made for this service, clearing brokers recoup their expenses through the interest rates that are paid and received. They need to be relatively competitive in order to make the service viable but they are designed to cover at least all the financing costs that the broker incurs on behalf of the client. From the client's point of view it makes the settlement process much more efficient and in particular reduces bank charges and administration for foreign transactions.

Treasury management

The efficient management of the margin calls is essential for several reasons. As we have said, margin, and the collateral used to cover it, is vital to controlling risk. From a regulatory point of view, the efficient management of margin calls enforces disciplines on the operations team. For instance, the clients clearing broker must make good the non-receipt of collateral from a client by utilizing its own funds.

We have already mentioned that the clearing houses have different rules about how margin is calculated and what is acceptable as cover. With a variety of acceptable collateral the clearing broker has to carefully assess the most efficient means of meeting the margin call at each exchange or with the clearing broker's agent used on an exchange. In addition to these issues the clearing broker will also find that for certain exchanges, the clearing house will margin the members on a net basis, i.e. offset the long and short positions in the client account. The broker, of course, will charge the client the full rate for the positions they have, thus creating a potential excess of collateral. If this excess is cash, the ability to effectively perform the treasury management function can provide important additional revenue.

However, an effective treasury management function is dependent on accurate and timely information about the margin calls from clearing houses/agents, the acceptable collateral, the margin calls for clients and the way in which the calls are to be covered, as well as what excess funds might be available. The client side of the process is particularly important as the broker may be, or need to be by commercial considerations, prepared to accept collateral from the client that cannot be used by a clearing house or agent and which cannot be transferred to the broker. In this situation the clearing broker must use their own means of covering the margin and pass on a funding charge to the client. The client would need to consider the merits of paying this charge in relation to the interest gained on cash utilized elsewhere.

Interest rate calculations

The disciplines associated with treasury management also include the constant monitoring of interest rates and the setting of the rate that the client will receive. If this is not performed accurately and in a timely manner, it is quite possible over the course of a year to reduce possible income and even, with clients that have complicated positions, to have lost money. A simple example is where excess funds on deposit were receiving, say, $5\frac{1}{4}\%$ and the client was being paid $4\frac{3}{4}\%$. The rate for the deposits falls to 5% but the operations area is not told to change the client rate.

The issue becomes more of a problem where the client has margin calls in, say, US\$, Euros and Australian dollars, but is covering the margin call with sterling. The client may be charged a debit interest on the 'overdrawn' currencies and receive credit interest on the sterling. The funding costs must be carefully monitored so that the respective debit and credit rates applied to the client accounts are correct in relation to any credit rates and funding costs incurred by the broker.

From the client's point of view margin and treasury management implications in respect of costs to the fund, cash utilization, foreign exchange risk, etc. may well become extremely important as their use of derivatives grows. In terms of control, the client will need to check the interest calculated and posted to the client accounts on a monthly basis. It is very important to check the accuracy of the interest rates charged and paid by the broker.

Using derivatives in investment management

Introduction

There are numerous ways in which derivative products are used in investment decisions. The house style, conditions, objectives and relevance to the business requirement determine strategies and product selection. Other key issues include liquidity, counterparty risk, and the regulatory environment. In this section we look at some basic examples of different ways of using derivatives.

Insight

Basic illustration of derivatives use in asset allocation
A fund manager has a portfolio made up of equity shares in the USA and the UK, gilt stocks and cash. The current ratio is 40% of the fund is invested in US equities, 20% in UK equities, 20% in gilt stock, 10% in Japanese stock and 10% cash.

The fund manager believes that the US equity market is due a fall and that Japan will rise. He expects this to occur in the next six to eight weeks and can adjust the balance of the portfolio by selling US shares and purchasing stocks in Japanese-based companies. He will need to research the markets then undertake several transactions and therefore it may take some time to achieve. Commission fees will be incurred for each transaction.

Alternatively the fund manager can use derivatives, in this case index futures, to gain and reduce exposure to the respective markets. He will sell S&P Index futures contracts and purchase Nikkei Index futures. If he is correct in his assumptions the sale of the S&P futures will offset the fall in price of the US stocks he holds while the Nikkei futures will rise, enabling the fund to participate in the increase.

There are several advantages for the fund manager:

- The futures transactions are very quick to effect and there is less commission, typically 2% for equities against 0.2% for futures.
- Exposure adjustment is immediate, reducing the risk of loss because of the market moving before shares can be sold/bought.
- The futures transactions can be quickly reversed if the assumptions are wrong.
- The fund manager can effect the actual sale/purchase of shares when ready.

Watch points

The portfolio must have congruence with the index product to be used otherwise the exposure will be incorrect and may result in gearing of the fund. This could breach internal/external regulations. There is also the need to calculate the value of the proposed allocation in the underlying currency of the index futures.

Income enhancement

A fund manager buys or holds significant amounts of equity stock. He is happy to sell some of these holdings at certain levels and would like to increase income over and above the dividend if possible. He looks to the traded options market.

He has purchased 500 000 BP shares at 600 p and will be happy to sell half of the holding if the stock rises more than 10%. The manager notes that the 650 call options expiring in two months can be sold for 25 p. He sells 250 contracts (1000 shares per contract) at 25 p.

The fund manager has given the right to someone to call the 250 000 shares at 650 p any time in the next two months in return for £62 500 (250 × 1000 × 25 p) of premium paid to him immediately. If the stock rises above 650 p he may have to deliver the stock at 650 p. If it does not rise above 650 p he will not have to deliver the stock.

In the first scenario he has effectively sold the stock for 675 p (650 +25) which meets his criterion of selling on a 10%+ share rise. Note that his profit is restricted to the difference between 600 p and 675 p no matter to what price the stock rises.

In the second scenario he still has the stock but has received income of £62 500 or, looked at another way, he has reduced the purchase price to 575 p. This means he is protected against a fall to this level on half of his holding.

Hedging

The fund manager is reviewing the portfolio and is concerned that the UK stock market may fall in the short term. However, he does not wish to change the weighting in the portfolio. He is, therefore, not looking at an asset allocation or to sell stock and considers two possibilities. First, he can sell FTSE futures contracts which will provide him with a profit as the market falls, thereby offsetting the fall in value of the stocks. Second, he could buy a 3-month FTSE put option.

With the futures contracts the fund manager risks incurring a loss if the market should rise until he decides to close the position. With the put option he can determine how much the 'insurance' against a fall in the market will cost and has the comfort that if the market should rise he will never pay more than the original cost of the option.

Index stands at 6960 on 3 January. The March futures contract is trading at 6975. The FTSE Feb 6950 put is quoted at 50 p.

Example

Scenario One
Fund manager sells 2 FTSE futures contracts @ 6975.

Market *rises* to 7010 by mid-February and the fund manager decides the market will not fall and buys two contracts at 7050 to close the position.

Outcome – the hedge has cost the fund manager 2×75 points or 150 ticks $(7050–6975) \times £5 = £1500$.

Example

Scenario Two
The fund manager buys 2 Feb 6950 puts @ 50 p

Market rises to 7010 by mid-February.

The 6950 puts are priced at 10 p.

Outcome – The hedge has cost the fund manager £1000 in option premium paid to open the position. If he closes the position by selling the put option he receives £200, a net cost of £800 excluding dealing fees.

Both strategies gave protection against a *fall* in the market. The put option restricted the cost of the hedge against a *rise* in the market. However, bear in mind that while there is a loss on the futures position as the index rises, the value of the stock has increased to compensate. With the option, the rise in the stock prices accrues to the portfolio once the £1000 outlay has been compensated for.

These are very simplistic examples and the decision on whether to use futures or options to hedge a portfolio or stock will be made taking into account many factors. In both cases the position could be quickly closed out if desired.

In the above examples we have seen how the fund manager wants to disperse or minimize the impact of risk on his portfolio. Others, of course, want to take on risk to profit from expected movements in price.

Speculator

A speculator believes that BP, which is currently at 600 p, will rise in the next few weeks. He has approximately £60 000 to invest. He could purchase 10 000 shares at 600 p or in the traded option market he could buy 250 of the 650 p call option contracts for 25 p or £62 500.

The call options give him an exposure to 250 000 shares, so if the BP stock price rises as he expects his potential profit far exceeds the amount he would make buying 60 000 shares yet he has made the same outlay.

If the stock price goes to 700 p, the 650 p call options would be worth at least 50 p so he would sell them for £125 000 for a profit of £62 500. Had he bought the 10 000 shares he would sell them for £70 000 for a profit of £10 000. (The characteristic of derivatives which enables a far greater reward for the same, or much smaller, initial outlay is often called *gearing*.) However, if the stock price fails to rise or indeed falls, he would risk losing all his £60 000 if he buys the options.

> ### Example
>
> If the stock falls to 575 p by the expiry of the options, the 650 p options are worth nothing. However, if he had taken a conservative view and only bought the 10 000 BP stock, although it is showing a loss, it is still worth £57 500.

The speculator therefore wants to assume risk for potentially much higher rewards.

Equity derivatives

Equity derivatives have seen very significant growth in recent years and it is worth looking at these products in more detail.

Product background

Since the first contract was introduced in 1982 on the Kansas City Board of Trade, stock index futures have been among the fastest-growing futures contracts. They have become so popular that in a number of cases the volume of futures market trading significantly exceeds trading volumes in the underlying cash market.

The first important contract, the S&P 500 contract traded on the Chicago Mercantile Exchange and launched in January 1983, is still the most heavily traded index futures contract. The Osaka Stock Exchange's contract on the Nikkei 225 index is also heavily traded.

Volumes in the established contracts continue to grow. At the same time, new derivatives exchanges are being set up around the world and are developing their own index futures contracts.

Recap on the product characteristics

A future is a legally binding agreement and an obligation between a buyer and seller to take delivery of/or make delivery of an underlying asset (in this case a stock index) on a particular date in the future at a price to be agreed today. A stock index contract allows investors and speculators to buy or sell the index at a fixed level. The seller, or 'short', has to deliver it at that level. However, futures contracts are rarely held to maturity. They are generally offset prior to settlement by an equal and opposite transaction before maturity.

With stock index futures it is almost impossible to buy or sell the underlying 'commodity' at maturity since the underlying 'commodity' is the stock index. Stock index contracts are therefore always 'cash settled'. When the contract matures, if the index is above the price at which the futures contract was bought, the seller, instead of having to deliver the index at the contract price, simply will have paid the buyer the cash difference between the index price and the contract price. If it is lower, then the buyer pays the cash difference. So an index futures contract is an agreement to buy or sell the cash value of the index at a future date.

Pricing

The price of a futures contract depends on the level of the index and the basic trading unit of the contract. For the S&P 500 futures traded on the CME, the unit is $250 for every index point; for the Nikkei 225 contract traded in SGX the unit is ¥500 × the index; for the FT-SE-100 contract on LIFFE it is £10 for every index point. So, if the FT-SE 100 index stands at 6000, the value of 1 FT-SE contract would equate to £60 000 (£10 × 6000). In practice, 6000 will not be the market price of the FTSE futures contract as there are important differences between the purchase of an index futures contract and that of the underlying basket of stocks.

The holder of the basket of stocks will receive dividend income but the holder of the future does not and should therefore be compensated for the loss of dividend income by a corresponding discount in the futures price. Higher expected dividend levels will lower the fair value of the futures contract since the holder of the futures does not receive the dividends.

Buying the basket of stocks involves payment of the full cost of the securities immediately whereas the purchaser of the futures contract only has to pay a small percentage of the cost of the securities (as his deposit or 'margin') initially, and so can earn interest on the remainder. The purchaser of the futures contract has only to pay a small percentage of the cost of the securities (as his deposit or 'margin') initially, and so can earn interest on the remainder. The purchaser of the futures should therefore be willing to pay a premium for the futures which will be offset by the interest received during the lifetime of the contract. The higher money-market rates, the higher the fair value of the futures. The longer maturity the contract, the greater this benefit will be and so the greater the premium. The higher the index level, the greater the cost of buying the underlying shares, and so the greater the carrying costs will be reflected in a greater fair value premium.

A simple formula for the calculation of fair value is as follows. It does not take into account the present valuing of futures dividends and incorporates individuals' expectations of dividend increases and interest rates.

$$Fv = \textit{spot index level} + \textit{cost of carry}^1$$

where
cost of carry = spot index level $\times$ (i/100–y/100) $\times$ d/365
$\quad\quad\quad\quad$ i = interbank rate
$\quad\quad\quad\quad$ d = the number of days from settlement day for the day of trade to the settlement day for the expiry date of the contract
$\quad\quad\quad\quad$ y = percentage annual yield of FTSE 100 Index

Assuming an index level of 6000 on 3 January, the first business day of the year, a forecast yield on the index of 4.1% and a 3-month interbank rate of 7.25%, the above formula can be used to calculate a fair value for the March FTSE future:

$$\text{Fair value}^1 = 6000 + 6000 \times (7.25/100 - 4.1/100) \times 66/365$$

$$= 6000 + 6000 \times (0.0725 - 0.041) \times 0.18$$

$$= 6000 + 34.02 \text{ or } 6034 \text{ (to nearest tick)}$$

If interest rates are generally higher than dividend yields, the futures generally trade at a premium to the underlying index. This premium is determined by comparing the interest that would be earned by

---

[1] *Source*: LIFFE FTSE Indices booklet.

buying futures with the dividends that would be paid on the underlying securities during the remaining life of the contract. This gives what is known as the 'fair value' of the futures contract.

This is a benchmark, not an absolute number, since different players in the market will have different expectations of unknown future dividends and different funding assumptions. Also the above formula is simplistic in the sense that the dividends that are to be paid in the future are not discounted to a present value.

Supply and demand factors will also affect the price, making the traded price differ from fair value. A future is expensive when it is at a premium to fair value and cheap when it is at a discount to fair value. The difference between the actual level at which the futures trade and the theoretical fair value is sometimes known as the 'value basis'. Each contract also has a minimum price change, known as the tick size. For example, the tick size for the FT-SE contract is 0.5 index points or £5.

Product uses

Stock index futures are an extremely flexible tool. Fund managers can use them to protect the value of a portfolio in a falling market; to provide a leveraged investment at a time of bullish sentiment; to enhance yields; to allocate assets easily, cheaply and quickly; and to track the performance of indices.

Market-makers in equities can use futures to hedge their exposure to a diversified trading book. Traders and speculators can use them to obtain maximum gearing for their gambles on market direction and arbitrageurs can use them to take advantage of pricing anomalies.

Investment/hedging

An investor who believes that the market as a whole will rise can buy exposure to the market in one trade by buying the requisite number of futures contracts rather than the individual equities. For example, an investor deposits £100 000 with his broker and buys 25 FT-SE 100 contracts at 5990 (equivalent to a £1 497 500 investment in the index, i.e. 25 contracts × £10 × 5990). Against this position, he has to put up a margin of, say, £2500 per contract (= £62 500). Some weeks later, after several rises and falls in the market the index has risen to 6040.

The investor decides to close out his position by selling 25 contracts (now equivalent to an investment of £1 510 000). His margin is returned and he makes a £12 500 profit (25 contracts × 50 points or 100 ticks (6040–5990) × £5 tick value).

A fund manager who is bearish and wishes to take a naked short position, or who has an underlying portfolio of shares whose performance is correlated with the index and whose value he wishes to protect against falls in the market, can sell futures contracts. In the latter case, of a short futures position against an underlying portfolio, the investor removes market risk from his total position and he will profit or lose to the extent that his portfolio out- or underperforms the underlying asset.

Gearing/speculation

An investor with a bullish view on the market movements can gear up by going long stock on futures. Depending on the particular contract, it can be possible to double positions (and so profits/losses) by paying out just 15% of the value of an existing portfolio.

Arbitrage trading

When the market price of a future differs significantly from its fair value, stock index arbitrage can be used to profit from the mispricing. If the future is trading at a premium to fair value the arbitrage involves buying the stocks which make up the index and selling the futures. The cost of holding the shares net of dividends received is included in the fair value of the future and consequently an investor holding shares and short an expensive future will be left with a profit after holding costs if he holds the position to expiry.

Conversely, if the future is trading at a discount to fair value (as it does typically) the arbitrageur can sell the shares which make up the index and buy the cheap future to lock in the undervaluation.

In practice, this arbitrage is limited by the cost of dealing. Futures prices have to differ from fair value by a certain amount before arbitrage is possible.

Asset allocation

Investment opportunities often arise quickly and usually unpredictably. Fund managers wishing to gain from such advantages would traditionally have had to liquidate all or part of their existing holdings. This would be costly, time consuming and possibly contravene their trust deeds.

Index futures contracts offer a cheap, quick and liquid method of shifting exposure from one market to another.

Index tracking

Few active stock pickers outperform their given index over the long term. An investor whose aim is to match the performance of a given index without the cost and difficulty of buying the underlying basket of shares can simply buy and roll over futures positions to give the exposure he requires. More complex futures-related trades are possible in which futures are used in combination with other instruments to enhance yields or reduce risk.

Summary

Index derivatives offer considerable flexibility and on many markets have sufficient liquidity for fund managers to make use of them. In addition to the flexibility there are potential cost savings over use of underlying securities on deal commissions and custodial charges. The futures transactions to some extent remove risk of price distortion that can affect the portfolio if heavy lines of buying or selling in individual equities were to take place. However, the use of index futures to hedge or for asset allocation can only be valid if the index and the underlying portfolio have sufficient correlation. If they do not the effect will be to create higher exposure and gearing of the portfolio.

OTC derivatives

Introduction

Over-the-counter derivatives are a large market, estimated by the International Swaps and Derivatives Association (ISDA) as being in trillions of US dollars in value. The combined OTC and exchange-traded markets can reasonably be said to be the largest market in the world. How do OTC derivatives differ from exchange-traded products?

We have seen how exchange-traded products are standardized into contracts such as futures or options and that they are actively traded in the secondary market, i.e. someone who buys a futures contract can sell it in the market to someone else. However, the standardization of the contracts does cause some problems when it comes to their use as hedging instruments as the amount of an asset to be hedged is often different from the size of the derivative contract which is, of course, fixed by the standardization process. Also the hedger may want to hedge the position for, say, 12 months and the asset may be a combination of different classes of the asset.

Example

A fund manager has a portfolio of UK equity shares in a combination of FTSE 100 stocks and smaller companies and wants to hedge the portfolio for 12 months. The value of the portfolio is £2 425 000 and the FTSE 100 index future is currently trading at 5823.5. If the fund manager decides to use the FTSE 100 index future there are some problems. First, the most liquid contract will be the nearest maturity, a maximum of 3 months away. Therefore the futures position will need to be 'rolled' over through different maturities in the course of the 12-month period. Second, the FTSE 100 index future is based on the 100 stock index and will therefore move in price according to the movement in the 100 stocks and will not therefore take into account the change in value of the smaller companies not in the index. The hedge correlation is therefore not right. Therefore the number of contracts required to hedge the portfolio would be:

$$\text{Portfolio}/£10 \times \text{index point} = 2\,425\,000/£10 \times 5823.5$$

$$2\,425\,000/58\,235 = 41.64 \text{ contracts}$$

You cannot trade 41.64 contracts so the fund manager must trade either 41 or 42 contracts. In either case the portfolio is not precisely hedged.

It is because of these kind of issues that hedgers often look to arrange an over-the-counter deal with a counterparty, usually a bank if it is a financial product, that can be tailored to meet the precise hedging requirement. On the other hand, the fund manager knows that there is a counterparty risk in an OTC transaction and there is no clearing house guarantee, possibly a capital adequacy issue as a result and that the position cannot usually be traded out of if the fund manager changes his mind.

Therefore both OTC and ETD derivatives can and often are used by the same organization and the choice will depend on the strategy, risk

Table 5.1 OTC and ETD derivatives

Characteristic	Derivative product	
	OTC	ETD
Contract terms	Tailored, negotiated, flexible and confidential	Standardized quantity, grade, maturity
Delivery	Negotiable dates and very often go to delivery	Defined delivery dates, terms but majority of contracts are closed out before delivery
Liquidity	Negotiated so can take time and can be limited by available counterparties	Usually very good for main contracts
Credit risk	Risk is with counterparty although some OTC products are now cleared by clearing houses Collateral is also used to reduce the risk	Clearing house becomes counterparty to all trades and manages risk through daily revaluations and margin calls

appetite, liquidity, cost and ability to close the position if desired (see Table 5.1).

With the terms of OTC derivatives being totally negotiated, the operations function is different from that of the exchange-traded products. Instead of standardized settlement processes and procedures such as daily variation margin calls we have periodic or event-driven settlement. We can illustrate this as we look at some of the products traded over-the-counter in more detail.

Forward rate agreements

A forward rate agreement (FRA) is an agreement to pay or receive, on an agreed future date, the difference between a fixed interest rate at the outset and a reference interest rate prevailing at a given date for an agreed period. FRAs are transacted between buyers who agree to the fixed rate and sellers who agree to the floating rate or benchmark. The benchmark rate will be, for instance, the London Inter Bank Offered Rate (LIBOR) and the settlement is calculated using a formula.

Example

Suppose a manufacturer needs to borrow £5 million in 1 month's time and needs the loan for a period of 3 months. Concerned about interest rates rising, the manufacturer decides to buy a FRA that will fix the effective borrowing rate today as they have no wish to borrow the money now when it is not needed.

The terms of the FRA are that the fixed rate is 7.25% and the benchmark is LIBOR. It will start in one month's time and finish three months later and would be known as a 'one v four' FRA

In one month's time the calculation of the settlement of the FRA can take place. The prevailing LIBOR at 11.00 am is used and let us assume this was 7.5%. The formula used to calculate settlement is:

Notional principal amount × (fixed rate − LIBOR) × days in FRA period/days in year divided by (1 + (LIBOR × days in FRA period/days in year))

Calculation:

£5 000 000 × (0.0725 − 0.075) × 91/365 over (1 + (0.075 × 91/365))

= **£3059.23**

The LIBOR rate was higher than the fixed rate so the buyer (the manufacturer) receives this amount from the seller. There is no exchange of the £5 million, the manufacturer will borrow the money from a lending source and the money received from the FRA will offset the higher borrowing costs of around 7.5%. Had the LIBOR been lower than the fixed rate, the manufacturer would have paid the difference to the seller but, of course, would borrow the money at a lower rate. The manufacturer 'locked' in a rate of 7.25% for their planned future borrowing. As far as settlement is concerned, the amount due is known on the settlement date, the date at which the FRA period starts (1 month's time) and the calculation period is known (3 months).

Unlike most transactions that settle on maturity a FRA can be settled at the beginning of the calculation period. The amount is present values or discounted to reflect the interest that would accrue if the amount paid was deposited to the end of the FRA period.

Swaps

Swaps are products that, as the title implies, involve the swapping of something. This can be, for instance, interest rates (an interest rate swap is abbreviated to IRS), currencies, equity benchmarks against an interest rate or commodities.

An IRS would be an agreement to swap or exchange, over an agreed period, two payment streams each calculated using a different type of interest rate and based on the same notional principal amount. The exchange of cash flows originating from, say, a fixed rate and a floating rate would be called a 'plain vanilla' or 'vanilla' interest rate swap.

By using swaps, a company can fix interest rates in advance for a specific period, typically 3 years to 10 years.

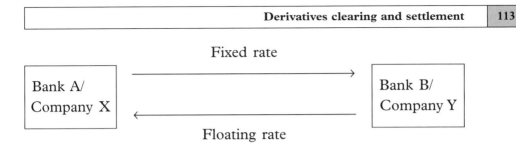

During the life of the above swap (known as the *term*) there will be an exchange of the netted payment flows at *payment date*, calculated at what is known as *reset dates*, i.e. semi-annually, annually and valued against the benchmark rate(s).

The payments cannot be netted at each reset date if the payment dates are different, i.e. the fixed is paid annually and the floating semi-annually. The IRS will be transacted to start at a forward date and will run for the agreed period. The start date is known as the *effective date* and the end date is known as the *termination date*.

The floating rate is reset at the effective date for the next period and then at reset dates for the next period throughout the term of the swap.

Example

Suppose Company X currently pays a floating rate of interest, say LIBOR + 0.4%, for a loan of $10 million over 5 years. Concerned that rates will rise the treasurer wants to change the payment flow to a fixed rate but is unable to alter the terms of the loan.

Company X approaches Bank B and agrees a 5-year IRS the terms of which are that Company X will pay 6.3% fixed, paid annually on an ACT/360 basis, and receive LIBOR semi-annually on an ACT/360 basis

At the beginning of the swap LIBOR is 6%. At the end of the first 6 months the floating-rate payment is:

$10 000 000 × 6.00% × 181/360 = $301 667 which is paid by Bank B to Company X

Note: there is no netted payment against the fixed rate flow for the period as the terms state that the settles are annually.

At the beginning of the next 6 months LIBOR is 6.25% and after 6 months the payments are:

Floating: $10 000 000 × 6.25% × 184/360 = $319 444 (due by Bank B to Company X)

Fixed: $10 000 000 × 6.30% × 365/360 = $638 750 (due from Company X to Bank B)

This time the settlement can be netted so that Company X pays $319 306 to Bank B.

In this IRS Company X has a risk as their view on interest rates over the next 5 years may be wrong and rates might actually fall, not rise. By agreeing to pay a fixed rate, in this case 6.3%, their cost of borrowing may be much higher than it would have been if they had entered into the swap.

As an alternative strategy the treasurer may have entered into a **swaption**. This is an option to enter into a swap. Like all options, it gives the treasurer the right, but not an obligation, to enter into the swap at some stage. As this is an OTC transaction the precise terms of the swaption and the cost of buying it will be negotiated.

Currency swap

A currency swap is an exchange of a series of cash flows in one currency for a series of cash flows in another currency, at agreed intervals over an agreed period, and based on interest rates. It is possible to have a combination of fixed and floating rates in two currencies in a currency swap:

- Fixed interest in one currency to floating rate in another
- Fixed interest in one currency to fixed interest in another
- Floating rate in one currency to floating interest in another

In a single-currency interest rate swap as described above there is no exchange of the principal amount. However, with a currency swap there is usually an exchange of the principal amounts at the beginning and end of the term at a rate agreed at the beginning.

Remember, this is an OTC transaction so a currency swap can have an exchange of principal at the beginning or end or not at all. If, say, a UK company wants to expand business in the USA by providing an influx of capital and it can borrow money cheaper in the UK where it is well known to its bankers, it can enter into a currency swap whereby:

- It can borrow British pounds (GBP) on a floating-rate basis from its bank and swap the GBP for dollars with the swap counterparty. It will agree to pay a fixed rate of interest on the dollars and receive a floating rate of interest on the GBP, which it uses to pay the interest on the original GBP loan from its bank.
- It agrees to exchange the principal amounts at the beginning at an FX rate that is agreed and will therefore need to fund the repayment of the loan, which is a totally separate transaction from the swap, from its own resources.
- The dollars are given to the US business and the subsequent income stream pays the interest on the dollars, which is paid to

the swap counterparty. As we have said, the GBP interest received from the swap counterparty pays the interest on the loan.

- During the term of the swap, which will correspond to the loan duration, the payment streams will be settled on reset dates. They are not netted because they are in different currencies.

This type of swap has achieved for the company protection against foreign exchange movements during the period of the swap and protects against interest rate movement in the UK market rate during the period of its borrowing.

Options

OTC options are often called 'exotic' because, unlike the standardized exchange-traded product, they possess additional characteristics that change the relatively simple call and put outcomes. As the terms are negotiated they are, of course, very flexible.

Common OTC options include:

- **Calls and puts** with specific amounts and duration, e.g. a £1 million, 2-year call option on the FTSE 100 index at a strike of 6005.2 (exchange-traded FTSE 100 Index options on LIFFE are listed with 9-month duration and a fixed unit of trading and strike prices)
- **Interest rate guarantee (IRG)**, which is an option on a FRA
- **Swaption**, which is an option on a swap
- **European, American** and **Bermudan** style options which have different exercise characteristics, i.e. on expiry, any time, specific times
- **Asian or average rate or average price options**, which use a different benchmark from the price of the underlying asset on expiry to determine if they are in- or out-of-the-money, e.g. the average price of the underlying over the last month

- **Barrier options** which is a general term for a family of options which are either cancelled or activated if the underlying price reaches a pre-determined level. They are also known as *knock-out*, *knock-in* or *trigger* options
- **Caps and floors** which are a series of 'rollover' rates agreed whereby the difference in rates is paid, if applicable at the time of the rollover
- **Collars** which operate like ordinary options but have limits on the level at which the customer can deal at a better market rate than the underlying, in exchange for a lower premium

We also have **puttable** and **callable** swaps which allow the fixed-rate receiver and fixed-rate payer respectively to terminate the swap early. They are traded as European, American and Bermudan styles of exercise right. Other products traded OTC are, for instance, forwards and warrants, structured products and credit derivatives.

Each of these separate products has slightly differing settlement processes. As with all derivatives there may be fixed times when a settlement event will occur and there may be settlement events that are triggered. Once again the database becomes crucial to the operations team.

Settlement of OTC products

The settlement of OTC derivatives is determined by the terms of the product as agreed by the two counterparties. There are, however, relatively standard settlement characteristics for particular products as we have already seen. Settlement events are triggered by such things as the effective date, reset date and payment date for swaps, the settlement date and calculation period for FRAs and the premium convention, exercise date and trigger events for options. For just about all derivatives there is also the maturity of the products when some event may occur as either mandatory or optional action. We also know that most products settle at the end of a period or on maturity with the exception of FRAs and IRGs where the settlement takes place by a discounted present value.

Key to the settlement of OTC products are the terms of the transaction. Unlike exchange-traded derivatives where the terms are stipulated by exchange regulation and contract specifications, each OTC trade is effectively a new set of terms, even though the product may be the same, i.e. a swap or option. OTC derivatives have documentation that helps to ensure that the terms of the derivative trade are agreed by the counterparties.

In the past this was a major obstacle to the use of OTC derivatives, as each trade had a separate agreement. This had to be vetted by the legal department and consequently delays and disputes caused considerable problems. The International Swaps and Derivatives Association (ISDA) has greatly helped to resolve the problems by developing standard documents for use by counterparties in OTC derivatives. The British Bankers Association also developed standard documentation for FRAs.

The standard documentation, known as a master agreement, can be supplemented with schedules, annexes and appendices that allow specific issues to be covered. ISDA master documents cover provisions for numerous aspects that are relevant and may need enforcing during the term of the agreement. These include:

- Contract currency
- Multi-branch facilities
- Payment provisions
- Default procedures
- Termination events
- Warranties, covenants and representations
- Tax indemnities
- Notices
- Assignment
- Legal jurisdiction
- Waiver of immunities

Also produced is what is known as a **confirmation**. This is provided as a detail of the trade terms rather than the general terms under which business is being transacted between the two counterparties. The confirm therefore lists key details for the operations teams as well as enabling the trade details to be reconciled. Confirmations should be issued by the operations team as quickly as possible so that the trade details can be reconciled. Equally, receipt of a confirmation from the counterparty, or a signed copy of a confirmation, sent to the counterparty should be chased as the confirm cannot be legally enforced unless both parties have acknowledged the details are the same or agreed.

Typically, two banks participating in a trade will send each other confirms while a bank and a client trade will result in a confirmation from the bank to the client which the client will sign and return. The role of the confirmation/documentation team in the context of OTC settlement is therefore vital.

The post-trade environment

There are many processes in the post-trade environment that are common to all transactions. These include:

- Trade capture and verification
- Position keeping
- Profit/loss analysis
- Confirmations and documentation
- Settlement
- Customer services
- Reconciliation
- Collateral management
- Risk management

Trade capture and verification requires considerable details to be input to the system. From a risk and control point of view the system must be capable of handling certain key information about a trade such as:

- Title of instrument traded
- Buy or sell (FRAs, options), pay or receive (swaps)
- Currency or currencies
- Amount or number of contracts (option) notional amount (FRAs, swaps)
- Exchange rate, price, rate of premium (two rates in the case of a fixed/fixed rate currency swap)
- Floating-rate basis/bases
- Exchange rate agreed for conversions of principal (currency swap)
- Strike price or rate (options)
- Trigger level (barrier option)
- Trade date and time
- Underlying asset (option, equity swap, etc.)
- Effective date
- Period (FRA)
- Settlement date(s)
- Maturity date
- Expiry date (option)
- Exercise styles and dates
- Day/year calculation bases (swaps)
- Physical/cash settled (options)
- Special conditions, e.g. for Asians options
- Trader
- Counterparty
- Deal method, e.g. screen, telephone

This list is not exhaustive and certain types of products, as they may have specific terms, will need additional information. In such cases where the full details cannot be recorded in the system then adequate manual processes and checks must be employed. However, yet again we see the need for an efficient, accurate and up-to-date database system and data management.

Certain transactions such as swaptions require both the option details and the swap underlying the option to be entered. Details of the settlement instructions, including netting if agreed, will also be input to the system and so will information such as the reference sources for fixings and possibly the documentation (ISDA, FRABBA) and governing law.

It is important that all these data are in the system so that key reports and information can be supplied to operations, dealers (positions and p/l), risk managers, general ledgers, reconciliation systems, etc.

Event calendar

The information about the transaction and the data in the database will also help to provide an event calendar that will enable operations to track the settlement events that will occur, e.g. resets, expiry, settlement dates. Some events are mandatory and/or automatic. This would include those related to barrier options, swaps, caps, collars and floors and FRAs. Others may require an instruction and/or decision by the dealer or client and this includes option exercise. However, some options are automatically exercised on expiry if they are in-the-money or termination (callable, puttable swaps).

Communication/information

Clearly the efficient settlement of OTC products requires a high degree of skill in managing the flow of information at, and immediately after, trading and then during the term of the transaction. Central to this is the confirmation. For a FRA a confirmation will typically be sent via SWIFT and would contain information shown in Table 5.2.

An IRS confirmation for a fixed/floating transaction would contain the information shown in Table 5.3.

Table 5.2 A confirmation sent via SWIFT

Confirmation from Mega Bank	To: InterBank Inc.
Buyer: **Mega Bank**	
Transaction date	19/06/2001
Effective date	21/06/2001
Terms	ISDA
Currency/amount	GBP 3 000 000
Fixing	19/09/2001
Settlement	21/09/01
Maturity date	21/12/2001
Contract period	91 days
Contract rate	5.79% pa on a actual/360 basis

Table 5.3 IRS confirmation for a fixed/floating transaction

Confirmation from Mega Bank	To: Interbank Inc
Interest rate swaps	
Transaction date	19/06/2001
Effective date	21/06/01
Maturity date	21/12/2001
Terms	ISDA
Currency/amount	UDS 5 000 000
We pay	5.76%
Frequency	Annual
Calculation basis	Actual/365
We receive	6-month LIBOR
Frequency	Semi-annual
Calculation basis	Actual/360

Source: Derivatives Management Services Ltd

There may be other pieces of information that can or will be added to this.

Other settlement issues

OTC products are heavily used and the number of organizations using them increases all the time. With some of the products being quite complex in their structure and certainly different in terms of the settlement process, the relationship with counterparties and clients in particular is important.

There will be many queries related to transactions, settlement, etc. and it is important that the operations teams within the two parties to the trade work closely together to resolve any problems quickly. Reconciliation is also a key issue and indeed reconciliation of the Nostro accounts in particular is important to ensure payments and receipts have been made. Any failure to receive expected payments may indicate a potential default. It is also important to mark to market OTC positions for profit/loss and to reconcile the positions against the dealers' records for exposure, limits and risk control management. The treasury management, including funding lines, cash flow management, etc., is crucial and so too is the reconciliation.

Collateral is a key risk control and where collateral has been taken as part of the risk management process it is vital to monitor that the collateral value is sufficient to cover the exposure risk. The key to whether collateral is required at all is the credit rating of the counterparty and the type of product. We need to be aware that with an OTC position, if a default should occur, there is no central guarantee provided by a clearing house unless the product is one of those cleared under, for instance, the LCH SwapClear facility. This is explained further below.

As a dealer may have the fixed side of a swap 'matched' between two counterparties, e.g. he is receiving a fixed rate from one counterparty and paying a lower fixed rate to the other, if the first counterparty defaults the dealer faces losses as the other counterparty must still be paid and it may cost the dealer more to replace the defaulting swap with another.

The amount of collateral needed will obviously rise or fall during the duration of the product. Making calls and returns is part of the operations role, as is the calculation of any interest due on cash collateral. Collateral helps to offset replacement cost and therefore reconciling its value and managing the process generally is vitally important.

As well as the event calendar there are other key static data issues to focus on, including the standing settlement instructions, client and product profiles, records of fixings, which need to be maintained in case of queries or for subsequent calculations.

Accounting and regulatory issues

Products like an IRS are shown as off-balance sheet items as there is an exchange of flows but no actual loan and deposit is made between the two counterparties. As far as profit and loss treatment is concerned then the profit and loss on trading should be realized immediately. The profit or loss on a hedge should take place simultaneously with the profit/loss on the item being hedged.

The UK Accountancy Standards Board requires banks to disclose information on interest rate risk, currency, liquidity, maturity, information on fair values and the effects of hedge accounting as described above. The FSA has reporting requirements related to transactions including options, and the European Union and Bank For International Settlements (BIS) have established guideline limits on risks, which each bank may take. In turn the local regulator such as the FSA in the UK will enforce these limits and may even make them stronger.

SwapClear

The introduction of a central clearing counterparty facility for OTC products including derivatives greatly helps to reduce the capital adequacy requirements associated with OTC transactions. The London Clearing House (LCH) launched SwapClear in September 1999 so that existing members that meet the membership criteria for SwapClear can have their OTC transaction cleared under the same principles used for exchange-traded derivatives, i.e. variation margin, initial margin. By having the OTC transaction cleared by LCH, an independent third party, the requirement to put up capital to cover counterparty risk is removed.

LCH also provide the same type of facility for other products through RepoClear and EquityClear. Other clearing houses such as CLEARNET for the Euronext market and EUREX do or will shortly offer similar facilities to clear OTC trades.

SwapsWire

SwapsWire is an electronic dealing system designed for the electronic online negotiation and trading of benchmark swaps and eventually options. Its objectives will be to provide lower transaction cost, fast transfer of deal information in a standard format and the facilitation of STP in OTC transactions. One significant advantage is that SwapsWire will provide the evidence of the deal and thereby removes the need for a confirmation to be sent. This will dramatically reduce the paperwork and process currently undertaken by OTC operations teams.

Chapter 6

Custody services

In this chapter we will look at the role of custodians and the services they provide to their clients. With sophisticated computer systems and a worldwide network of sub-custodians, global custodians are in a position to deliver a growing portfolio of services to their clients. Referred to by global custodians as either *core services* or *value-added services*, the range offered includes:

- The safekeeping of securities
- The maintenance of multi-currency securities and funds accounts
- The settlement of securities trades in domestic and foreign markets, on a free of payment or delivery versus against payment basis
- The collection of dividends, interest and principal amounts due for redemption on due date
- The exercising or selling of subscription rights and attending to other corporate actions
- The reporting of transactions completed and the periodical delivery of hardcopy statements of account
- Contractual or actual settlement date accounting
- Contractual or actual income collection
- Terminal or computer-to-computer links to pass on instructions and retrieve client information from the custodian's database
- Customized multi-currency reporting and performance information

- Securities borrowing and lending
- Assistance with withholding tax claims
- Handling/settlement of derivatives
- Briefings on specific countries, in particular on emerging markets
- Cash projection and cash management
- Ensuring that physical certificates and associated documentation are in good order.

From a global custodian's perspective, core services are those which are so standardized that there is not a great deal of scope for any particular global custodian to differentiate its service from that of another global custodian. Any fundamental changes and improvements will affect the industry as a whole.

Value-added services, on the other hand, provide the global custodians with the opportunity to offer a broader and different service to their clients, and in so doing, enhance the global custodians' standing within the marketplace and improve their fee-earning capabilities.

Settlement is, as we know, the final transfer of cash from the purchaser to the seller in exchange for the delivery of the securities to the purchaser. However, settlement conventions vary widely from country to country and especially in the areas of physical delivery and book entry transfer.

To illustrate the difference we can look at the situation for an equity transaction prior to the introduction of CREST in the UK and at how the ICSDs settle Eurobonds. In the UK prior to CREST an investor had to physically lodge the share certificate together with relevant transfer documentation with a London Stock Exchange processing office prior to settlement (Figure 6.1).

Eurobonds, held in electronic book entry form by Euroclear and Clearstream, are settled by Book Entry Transfer (BET). The securities

CREST TRANSFER

Above this line for Registrar's use

Counter Location Stamp	Barcode or Reference SDRN

Above this line for completion by the depositing system-user only.

	Consideration Money	Certificate(s) lodged with Registrar (To be completed by Registrar)
Name of Undertaking.		
Description of Security		
Please complete form in type or in block capitals.	Amount of shares or other security in words	Figures
Name(s) of registered holder(s) should be given in full: the address should be given where there is only holder. If the transfer is not made by the registered holder(s) insert also the name(s) and capacity (e.g. executor(s) of the person(s) making the transfer	In the name(s) of	Designation (if any) Balance certificate(s) required
Please Sign Here	I/We hereby transfer the above security out of the name(s) aforesaid into the name(s) of the system-member set out below and request that the necessary entries be made in the undertaking's own register of members. Signature(s) of transferor(s) 1. 2. 3. 4. A body corporate should execute this transfer under its common seal or otherwise in accordance with applicable statutory requirements.	Stamp of depositing system-user Date
Full name(s) of the person(s) to whom the security is transferred Such person(s) must be a system member.		Participant ID Member Account ID
Reference to the Registrar in this form means the registrar of registration agent of the undertaking, <u>not</u> the Registrar of Companies at Companies House.	CRESTCo Limited is delivering this transfer at the direction and on behalf of the depositing system-user whose stamp appears herein and does not in any manner or to any extent warrant or represent the validity, genuineness or correctness of the transfer instructions contained herein or the genuineness of the signature(s) of the transferor(s). The depositing system-user by delivering this transfer to CRESTCo Limited authorises CRESTCo Limited to deliver this transfer to registration and agrees to be deemed for all purposes to be the person(s) actually so delivering this transfer for registration. This form should be used only for a transfer of a certificated unit of a security to a CREST member to be held by a CREST member in uncertificated form. It should not be used for conversion of a unit held by a CREST member into uncertificated form. The CREST rules requires that this form be used for the transfer of a unit of a certificated security to a CREST member to be held by that member in uncertificated form. Any such transfer on this form is exempt from stamp duty.	

Figure 6.1 CREST transfer form

accounts of the seller and the buyer are credited and debited respectively. This process is widely used by the major clearing organizations like CREST. However, while markets are moving towards book entry transfer, it is worth remembering that a number of securities markets are still paper-based and in the UK there is the choice of either dematerialized or certificated settlement through CREST.

How and where else does settlement differ across the world? Look at the following examples that highlight some of the differences.

- *Rolling settlement versus fixed settlement dates* In the majority of worldwide securities markets, trades settle on a rolling basis, i.e. a fixed number of days after trade date in line with G30's Recommendation No.7.
- *The length of elapsed time from trade execution to trade settlement* G30 recommended that settlement of all types of securities should take place on at least a T+3 basis throughout the world. There are variations to this with, for example, transactions in Hong Kong settling T+2, the UK T+3 and T+5 in India

In theory, all securities transactions should settle on time and in accordance with local market conventions. This allows investors to make efficient use of their money, whether for funding a purchase or placing/reinvesting sale proceeds. In reality, the ability to settle securities transactions on time varies from country to country and within security types.

We have seen in the previous two chapters that there are many reasons why trades fail to settle on the due date, for example:

- Late/incorrect settlement instructions from a counterparty to the custodian or clearing agent
- Seller has insufficient quantity of securities to deliver either as a result of a failed purchase or, for example, a market-maker's business decision to go short (i.e. to sell securities that he does not have)
- Purchaser has insufficient funds to pay
- Certificated securities are not yet available from the registrar from a recent purchase to cover a sale: the registration process can take up to several months to complete.

While there are individual market mechanisms, (for example, buy-ins) to help resolve these failures, the result is that securities administration becomes inefficient, exposure to risk increases and costs rise. Buy-ins permit the purchaser to achieve timely settlement by purchasing the securities from another agent. The securities are delivered and the extra costs passed on to the original seller. In some Far Eastern markets the buy-in process is automatically generated by the market together with financial penalties and, in some circumstances, suspension of the offending broker's trading licence.

Custody providers seek to offer their clients services that ease the administration process even when problems with settlement occur. One such process concerns settlement accounting. In terms of settlement accounting, custodians would credit sale proceeds and debit purchase costs on whatever date the trade actually settled. This is known as *actual settlement date accounting (ASDA)*. The application of ASDA works in favour of purchasers as they will have the use of their funds for an extra few days and perhaps the opportunity either to earn interest or to place the funds on deposit for that period.

However, ASDA is a disadvantage for sellers who will be unable to use the funds until received. This can cause a knock-on problem where the expected funds were committed for other purposes on the original settlement date. Overall, ASDA in poorly performing markets handicaps the investor by making it difficult to manage cash flow requirements and cash positions effectively. Custodians have approached this problem by making a commitment to the investor that funds will be debited or credited for good value (in this case on the original settlement date). This is *contractual settlement date accounting (CSDA)*. It enables the investor to operate in the certain knowledge that the cash accounts will reflect the expected entries and balances. However, in one or more of the following circumstances the global custodian will protect himself from risk of non-performance of the trade by insisting on variations in its contractual commitments to the investor:

- CSDA is not offered in those countries which the global custodians consider to have a substandard settlement infrastructure.
- Investors' settlement instructions which have missed a deadline will be considered received the following day by some global custodians. In other words, either the CSDA value will be applied on a later date or ASDA will be applied.
- The global custodian retains the right to reverse cash entries in the event that trades remain unsettled after a particular length of time.
- CSDA on a sale will not be provided if there are insufficient securities to satisfy the delivery.

Whichever accounting practice is used, it is in the global custodian's interests (and the client's where ASDA is used) to apply pressure on the local stock markets and authorities to improve the settlement environment.

There are obviously procedures and processes in the provision of custody services that affect the custodian and the client. The principal objective in global custody provision is to pass an accurate and timely instruction from the client to the Central Securities Depository or clearing agent based in the country of the security via the global custodian and sub-custodian network, or vice versa (Figure 6.2).

Instruction from client to global custodian

There are numerous ways in which the client is able to send a settlements instruction to the global custodian. Traditionally this has been either manually or verbally.

Manual/verbal instructions

- Telephone instruction (with call-back from the custodian to the client) supported by a mailed confirmation from the client

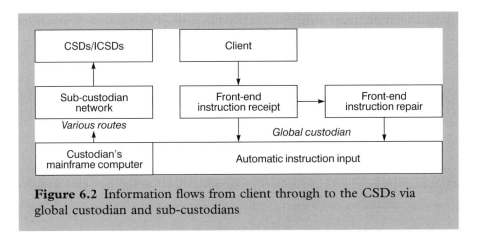

Figure 6.2 Information flows from client through to the CSDs via global custodian and sub-custodians

- Faxed instruction supported by a mailed confirmation from the client
- Written instruction duly authorized by one or more officers of the client
- Tested telex instructions in which the message is preceded by a series of digits uniquely identifying the instruction initiator to the receiving custodian and confirms to the custodian that the instruction may be acted upon. Usually, clients have the preparation of telexes automated within their systems.

However, these methods are in many ways inefficient and are not to be encouraged for the following reasons:

- Even though a telephoned instruction is called back correctly, there is no guarantee that the initiator of the instruction had the authority to issue the instruction
- Control is difficult to maintain in the absence of an effective and robust audit trail of the instructions
- It is not possible to authenticate with absolute certainty the location from which a faxed instruction was sent
- Written instructions can easily be delayed, mis-directed, or lost and the investor has no means of knowing if the instruction has been received until it is possibly too late to issue a replacement instruction.

All the above methods are to a greater or lesser extent time consuming and open to error and misuse. For obvious reasons the use of electronic instructions is now becoming the industry standard.

Electronic instructions

We can consider a generic process whereby the client enters instruction details into the global custodian's system. The software converts the instructions into electronic data files, which are then transmitted via a modem/telephone link to the global custodian's computer system.

Electronic transmission of instructions is preferable to manual methods for a variety of reasons:

■ The software applications and the hardware in which it resides can be protected by both physical and electronic methods such as locating the PCs in a secure environment in the office and only allowing access to those staff who have authorized system identification numbers and user passwords.
■ The preparation of electronic instructions is faster and more accurate and can be incorporated into a straightthrough processing (STP) environment.
■ More effective controls can be established with full audit trails generated by the software.
■ Data files can be retained by using the archiving capabilities of the software thus dispensing with the need to retain large quantities of paper files.

Instructions are also made between the global custodian and sub-custodian.

There are three main methods by which the global custodian is able to communicate with the sub-custodian. Which method is used depends to an extent on whether the sub-custodian is a branch of the global custodian or a third party:

- If there is an own-branch relationship and both global custodian and sub-custodian share the same systems technology, then trade instructions are transmitted through this medium.
- If the sub-custodian is a third party or an own branch without a common technology, then instructions will be translated into a suitable message format and transmitted electronically through a communication network known as SWIFT.
- Tested telex.

Then we have instructions from the sub-custodian to the settlement agent/CSD and the methods by which sub-custodian communicates with the settlement agents and CSDs are dependent on local market practices.

Custody problems occur. For instance there are a number of issues that affect the ability of a client to achieve timely settlement of overseas securities trades.

Following the initiatives by G30, ISSA and other industry participants, global settlement practices are improving and timescales shrinking. There is a danger that if the lines of communication between client and their global custodian, global custodian and sub-custodian and sub-custodian and local market fail to meet the new settlement standards then settlement performance will be compromised.

With the final objective of a T+1 settlement period, there is the problem of initiating a settlement instruction early enough to allow the global custodian to pass on the instruction to the sub-custodian and from there to the local market. There are, as we know, many markets that have T+3 settlement and some markets with shorter settlement date cycles. The global custodian receives the client's instruction and ensures that it is valid before passing it on to the sub-custodian. If this involves transferring the information from one system to another by a process of rekeying the data, then the risk of error and delay is high. Consequently, there is little time to correct any errors before settlement due date. The solution is based on the ability of the client to prepare and transmit a data file of information (i.e. the settlement instructions) to the local market without the need for either the global custodian or sub-custodian to rekey the data into another format. This is the STP concept and requires common technology standards at every stage along the communication chain.

Reporting requirements

The global custodian is able to offer settlement activity reports to the client in either hardcopy form or by data transmitted electronically to the client's system via a link. Electronic reporting provides the investor with the opportunity to extract only the information that is required. This is achieved by transferring the data from the custodian's system into the client's proprietary computer system and then the client sorting the information in any order, e.g. all trades on a particular settlement date, all trades in a particular security number, etc. to suit their requirements.

A fundamental service offered by custodians has always been safekeeping of securities. It is important to note that custody is an integral part of the investment process and a high level of confidence in the security of safe custody is indispensable in meeting investor protection objectives such as:

- Preventing misuse of investors' assets
- Safeguarding ownership rights

Global custodians and their clients must operate within the general laws of the countries in which they are based as well as complying with any regulatory obligations. For the global custodian, this can become a complicated exercise when entering into legal agreements with sub-custodians based in different jurisdictions.

The main regulator of the securities industry is the Financial Services Authority and the segregation of a client's assets from those of firm is a main part of the regulation. For securities that can be registered, the name of the investor is shown on the face of the certificate and reflected on the issuing company's register of shareholders. Private investors who do not use the services of a custodian for safekeeping purposes may have their holdings registered in their own names.

While this has the advantage that the beneficial owner can be readily identifiable (i.e. name on register), it does cause administrative problems for custodians who are appointed to look after the shareholdings of many investors. For example, all dividends, corporate actions, company announcements etc. will be sent directly to the shareholders' addresses, and not to the custodian. The custodian will arrange for its clients' registered securities to be registered in the name of a nominee company established by it specifically for that purpose.

Whether the shares are registered in the name of the investor or the nominee, making changes on the company share register can be a time-consuming process, especially in a certificated environment. Reregistration can take anything from a week up to several months to complete, depending on the particular country.

It is important to differentiate between legal ownership and beneficial ownership. Whoever's name is on the register has legal ownership of the securities. In the case of a nominee's name, the beneficial owner is the underlying investor, as shown in Table 6.1.

Table 6.1 Ownership of securities

Whose name is on company register?	Legal ownership held by	Ownership held by
Investor	Investor	Investor
Nominee	Nominee	Investor

For book-entry securities, there are no certificates so the holdings in these securities will be reflected by entries on a ledger statement.

The nominee company becomes the legal owner of the investments and its name appears on the issuing company's register of shareholders. Beneficial ownership is implied in this situation and it is the custodian's responsibility to maintain accurate records of the underlying beneficial owners.

There are two different approaches to the management of nominee holdings both of which provide a secure and effective custody environment. This can only occur so long as proper and continuous controls are operated by the custodian.

Pooled nominee system (omnibus)

Under this system, where all investors' holdings are registered in the same name (e.g. ABC Nominees Ltd), the entries on the share register and the certificates do not identify the actual beneficial owners.

Advantages of pooling

- Administration is simplified and risk of clerical error reduced.
- The settlement process is made easier as any certificate(s) may be delivered from the pool so long as the total does not exceed the number of shares actually held for the shareholder at the time of delivery.
- There is only one holding for the custodian to reconcile in respect of each issue (although there must be a subsequent reconciliation of this holding to the records of the underlying investors).
- It reduces the number of names that need to be maintained by the registrar on the company register.
- It provides anonymity for the investors except in cases where disclosure is required in accordance with the Companies Act 1985 s.212.

Disadvantages of pooling

Although it is prohibited, there is the risk that a custodian with poor controls might use the shares of one investor to settle trades of another when there are delays in the settlement system.

- It is difficult to establish beneficial ownership in the absence of comprehensive and up-to-date records.
- More time is required to allocate dividends, corporate actions proxy voting, etc., to individual investors.

Within the nominee approach there is also the facility for individual designation.

Individual designation (segregation)

Under a system of individual designation within a nominee name, individual beneficial owners are identified by the addition of a designation. This designation, which can be a unique reference rather than a name, will also be reflected in the issuing company's register.

Advantages of individual designation

- Beneficial owners are more easily identifiable from the company register and the share certificates.
- Reconciliation of shareholdings to investors' balances is more straightforward.
- Time spent allocating dividends, etc. is reduced.
- The risk of using the balance of one investor to settle the trades of another is reduced.
- Individual designation will facilitate the process of establishing claims for securities in a default situation.

Disadvantages of individual designation

- There is the risk that the holdings of one investor might be incorrectly designated under the designation of another investor.

- It might be unsuitable for a custodian with many holdings over a wide client base. This would make the administration of such a client base difficult to manage and costly to operate.

Let us now turn to reconciliation, a key control and an important issue not just for the custodian but also for the client. Securities reconciliation is a control that seeks to establish that balances of assets beneficially owned by one party agree with the balances of the same assets held on behalf of the beneficial owner by another party. This issue is discussed further in a separate book in the series called 'Controls, Procedures and Risk'.

It is obvious that adequate reconciliation should be a part of a firm's procedures. This is reinforced by regulation and, for instance, in the UK the rules oblige a firm to reconcile all holdings not evidenced by physical certificates at least every 25 business days. Physically held securities need to be checked only every six months.

When in the reconciliation process there are discovered positions that do not agree, or reconcile, they must be queried in order to establish the reasons why this is the case. Reasons for a reconciliation problem can range from clerical error to unsettled trades and on to unauthorized use/fraudulent misappropriation of the assets.

Global custodians and their investors reconcile their positions by electronically matching their respective securities balances, outstanding trades and corporate action events and, in so doing, produce an exception report highlighting only those securities which require remedial action.

To enable reconciliation to take place, both the client and global custodian require asset listings that can be available in hardcopy format or downloaded/accessed from the custodian's systems. The information on the asset listings usually indicates:

- Investor account identification
- Security name
- Security identification number

- Quantity of securities (ledger and settled balances, outstanding receipts/deliveries balances)
- Name of depository in which security is held
- Valuation in currency of security
- Valuation in base currency of investor

Every reconciliation is important. Problems associated with reconciliations that are not carried out correctly or are incomplete become magnified when there are other events that might occur, such as corporate actions.

Corporate actions

Corporate actions is a collective term used to describe the entitlements of any securities holder. They can be divided into those that require no action from the investor (e.g. a bonus issue) and those that do call for the investor to make a decision (e.g. a rights issue).

For the global custodian, and the client, there are a number of issues to take into consideration when dealing with events that require the investor either to make a decision or to take no action at all. Disregarding the risk factors, a trade that fails to settle on time will eventually settle. There might be penalty interest to pay and possible delays in other related trades; the trade nevertheless still stands. The overriding factor in such cases where a settlement has failed but a corporate action is announced is to ensure that the rightful owner receives the benefit arising from the corporate action. All parties in the information chain must receive instructions and be required to take appropriate action before the deadline expires. A missed corporate action is irretrievable and internal controls must be able to recognize this possibility. Incomplete reconciliation of actual positions and settlements pending, including failed settlements, means the likelihood of missing a corporate action is that much greater.

It is also important to record details of corporate actions in the ledgers on the correct date to ensure that the fund or portfolio is priced correctly.

The prime source of information covering registered securities is the issuing company or its agent. The global custodian has to rely on the sub-custodian network to gather this information and pass it on with a minimum of delay and, where appropriate, translate it into the relevant language for the client. Secondary sources of information would be journals like the *Financial Times* or *Wall Street Journal*. However, these secondary sources become primary sources for bearer securities where the issuing companies are unable to communicate directly with their shareholders and bondholders.

The quality and source of information about corporate actions is important otherwise problems will be experienced. Specialist information suppliers such as the *Derivative and Dividend Directory* are often utilized by firms.

With a corporate action it is also important to ascertain who is entitled to the benefit. The amount of benefit due to an investor is determined by reference to the quantity of shares each investor holds on a record date. The record date is determined by and announced by the issuing company. The local market will establish a date (the *ex date*) that is used to determine whether the buyer or seller of shares is entitled to receive the benefit.

Figure 6.3 illustrates a dividend payment, but equally there are specific deadlines and dates in virtually all types of corporate action. (We have covered the mechanics of record date etc. in Chapter 4.)

A problem arises when a purchaser who has bought shares before the ex date (i.e. is entitled to receive the benefit) does not have his name placed on the register before the record date. As the registrar is unable to recognize the new shareholder, the benefit is given to the previous shareholder (the seller), even though he is not entitled to it.

The global custodian must make sure that entitlements are received on a timely basis to avoid lost opportunities in trading. There should therefore be a mechanism in place to ensure that the correct

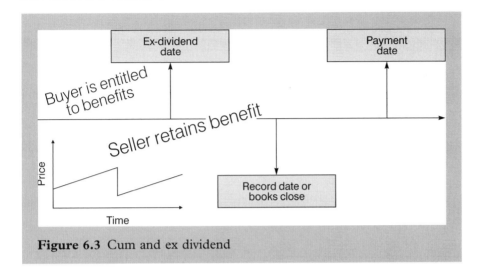

Figure 6.3 Cum and ex dividend

entitlements are received and, if not, claimed from the seller. It is the global custodian's duty to provide as much information as possible to enable the client to make the necessary decisions, to ensure that the information is accurate and to allow enough time for the client's instructions, where appropriate, to be relayed back to the company. As there is a variety of information types, it has not been easy for the global custodians to translate this into electronic message formats for the client. Instead, information on corporate actions has tended in the past to be sent by telex and mail. This situation is changing as the quality of information from the overseas markets improves. What are the implications of corporate actions for the client? The client will need to be given a deadline by the custodian by which to convey any instructions to the custodian and for the global custodian to pass them on to the local market. This can cause a problem for the client where, for instance, the fund manager or dealer might want to delay their decision until the last possible moment. This will, out of choice of course, be very close to the deadline stated in the local market rather than the global custodian's.

In this case the client's settlement department and the global custodian have to delay sending their respective instructions until the very last moment and, in so doing, risk missing the deadline. In this instance the client must accept full responsibility for a missed event if instructions are sent or arrive after the custodian's deadline.

Apart from global custodians ensuring that clients' instructions are passed on to the local market, they must also ensure that the benefit is received in good time. Where appropriate, market claims must be made to achieve this. As we have already noted, the clearing houses are often in a position to make claims for benefits automatically when a settlement occurs.

We also know from the previous chapters that there are various types of corporate action. Let us recap and expand a little on the issues for the custodian as corporate actions are a vital part of the overall settlement process for both the client and the custodian.

A benefit distribution is a distribution made by a company to its shareholders in the form of cash, securities or a combination of both in cases where an entitlement is a fraction of a share. Distributions are usually made in proportion to the investor's holding as at the record date. Cash benefits include the following.

Dividends on shares

Apart from when a trade has not settled by record date and a claim is necessary, the dividend process is straightforward and the shareholder would expect to receive the cash amount the dividend represents on or shortly after pay date. However, the speed with which the dividends are paid once the payment date has been announced varies considerably throughout the world. As part of the cash management process the client needs to know promptly when the cash in respect of the dividend is received.

Interest payments

As we determined in Chapter 3, an interest payment is a cash payment made to holders of debt securities including:

- Bonds and loan (fixed interest and floating rate)
- Foreign bonds and international bonds
- Convertible bonds

The rate of interest (the coupon) and the frequency of payment are determined within the original terms of issue of the debt. As the company's agent pays the interest on the dates specified by these terms, there is more certainty of value for both the global custodian and the investor.

The global custodians are in a position to offer a **contractual income collection service**. The client's cash accounts will be credited with good value a pre-determined number of days after the intended payment date. The delay is needed as it reflects the ability of the local market to make payment and therefore is crucial if the custodian is not to assume significant risk. Contractual income is generally offered in most countries (see Table 6.2).

Clients have the option to receive income either in the base or in the underlying currency of the security; either way the custodian will give good value.

Table 6.2 Countries offering contractual income

Australia	Hong Kong	Portugal
Austria	Ireland	Singapore
Belgium	Italy	South Africa
Canada	Japan	Spain
Denmark	Malaysia	Sweden
Finland	Netherlands	Switzerland
France	New Zealand	UK
Germany	Norway	USA

Source: The *dsc* Portfolio.

Repayment of capital

A capital repayment is a partial repayment of a company's issued capital. The company pays each shareholder a proportion of the value of the shares at the current market price. While the number of shares issued remains the same, the nominal value of each share is reduced by the amount of the capital repayment per share.

Stock benefits include the following.

Rights issues

A rights issue is an issue of additional shares offered by a company to its existing shareholders and in proportion to their existing shareholdings as at a record date. Shareholders are offered the right to subscribe for new shares on or before a pre-determined date in a ratio to their holdings at a price below the current market price.

The global custodian's first task is to provide all the clients who have a shareholding with full details of the issue including dates and payment amounts.

There are several options available to a shareholder:

- The nil-paid rights can be traded; or
- The rights can be accepted and paid for by making a cash payment (known as a call payment); or
- The nil-paid rights can be allowed to lapse, i.e. neither traded nor accepted; or
- Sufficient nil-paid rights can be sold and the proceeds used to pay the call on the remaining rights.

It is, therefore, most likely that the global custodian will have to give a series of different instructions to the company. All the clients' instructions must be received in time and accurately passed on to the company. As mentioned above, late or incorrect instructions will result with the global custodian, if at fault, making good the client's position. This may involve financial loss.

Capitalization

A company can recapitalize or restructure its capital. Among the alternatives, this may be to reduce the number of shares in issue or to reduce the price of the shares. To achieve the latter a capitalization event, more often called a bonus or scrip issue, takes place. This is the free issue of shares to existing shareholders in proportion to the shareholders' balances as at record date.

In this case, the client does not need to give any instructions. However, the global custodian should inform them of the issue as the number of shares will change. The share price will, however, alter as the overall market value of the shareholding remains the same.

Care must be taken in the finance and cash management areas as some bonus shares do not qualify for the next dividend payment. For the custodian and the client the records of the shareholding must be changed at the appropriate date. If this did not occur the portfolio would show a significant loss of value as the share price reduced but the number of shares held was not changed.

Example

A two-for-one bonus issue is announced. The shares are currently showing in the portfolio as:

1000 shares @ £30 value £30 000

After the bonus issue the share price will change to £10, i.e. three shares worth £30 instead of one share worth £30. If the portfolio is not updated correctly the result will be:

1000 shares @ £10 value £10 000

An incorrect valuation of £20 000.

Scrip dividends

Companies can use scrip dividends as a method of distributing profits in the form of shares instead of cash. The shareholder is offered the normal process of receiving the benefit in cash or given the option to receive shares.

In exactly the same way as for cash dividends, the entitlement to scrip dividends is based on shareholdings on the register as at record date. The number of shares offered takes into account the amount of dividend payable and the underlying market price of the shares. In most cases the scrip, if it is offered, is an option for the holder of the shares and therefore the global custodian must ensure that the client's instructions are obtained. If the decision is to take a scrip dividend then that action needs to passed on to the paying agent by the deadline. Although the company will usually pay the cash dividend in the absence of any instructions to the contrary, it is important to check the terms of the issue in case the basic offer is for scrip. In most cases, it is possible to issue standing instructions for future scrip dividends to be paid when offered.

Stock situations

Any event that changes the nature or description of a company's securities can be described as a stock event or situation. Stock situations are either optional, where the shareholder has a choice, or non-optional, where the shareholder is required to accept the company's decision for the change.

For the global custodian, there is the problem of collating sufficient information to allow the client to make a decision where appropriate, acting on the decision within the deadlines and timetable for the event and ensuring that the results of the stock situation are correctly received.

Take-overs, mergers and de-mergers

These are situations in which two or more companies are involved. A take-over is where a bidding company wishes to obtain a controlling interest in a target company. It is optional for the investor to the extent that he can accept or decline the offer within the deadline specified by the bidder.

If, in the terms of the offer, the bidder agrees to take over 100% of the company on condition that there is, say, a 75% acceptance level, then the remaining shares are compulsorily acquired, i.e. the situation becomes non-optional for those shareholders who did not accept the offer.

A merger is where two or more companies have agreed to merge their companies and create in effect a new company. As a result the share structure of each company will probably change and often the merged company will assume a new name. The merger, although recommended by the boards of the relevant companies, is still subject to acceptance by the shareholders at an AGM or specially convened extraordinary general meeting (EGM). This meeting will outline the new share structure and timetable. There may be both new shares and a cash element involved and from a specified date the new shares in the company are traded and existing shares cease to exist.

A de-merger results in an additional 'new' company being created and existing shareholders receiving some kind of benefit such as shares in the new company and possibly a cash payment too. Just like a merger, the shareholders will agree to a de-merger. For the custodian and client there is the need to get the information about the situation, agree to it or otherwise and then to receive any shares and or cash with a corresponding update to the portfolio

Conversions

Clients who are holders of convertible debt securities may wish to convert the debt into equity. The full terms for the conversion are specified at the original issue date and generally allow the investor the right to convert at pre-determined rates and times set by the company.

The actual conversion is optional except that the last possible date for conversion is itself non-optional, i.e. the debt is either redeemed for cash or automatically converted into equity according to the issue terms.

Warrant exercise

Whether or not to take up the shares that a warrant relates to is an option for the holder. The warrant gives the holders the right to 'exercise' the warrant in exchange for equity by making a subscription payment to the issuing company. If they are not exercised by the last possible date, the warrants expire worthless. In some cases the warrants can be bought and sold separately and there is therefore an alternative to exercise or abandonment on expiry. The custodian and client need to communicate prior to the last exercise and expiry date on the action to be taken with obvious consequences if this does not happen.

Pari passu lines of a security

This is an area that can cause many problems for the global custodian and investor alike. When a company issues new securities that are identical to existing securities already in circulation through, say, a rights issue, the new securities may for a while not be entitled to current benefits associated with the existing shares.

For instance, for a pre-determined period of time, the new securities do not qualify for a particular dividend or are subject to some other type of restriction (for example, they cannot count in any vote at the next general meeting of the company). Once this period is over, the two lines of securities are merged and become *pari passu*; they rank equal in all respects.

Until the two lines of securities become *pari passu* they are given separate security codes and in addition will trade at different prices. Both global custodian and investor must be aware of these differences and reflect the holdings accurately in the safekeeping records.

Redemptions and maturity

A redemption or repayment is a stock situation where the company repays its debt to holders in order to redeem part or all of the issued loan. We know that the redemption can be on a specific date, during a period or at the request/offer of the issuer or the holder of the security.

The redemption becomes non-optional at final maturity of the loan but prior to this any possible action to redeem early must be communicated to the client for a decision. In the case of bonds and loan stock that is bearer we know that the issuer can only make this possibility known either at the time of issue, i.e. a security might be issued as ABC Loan Stock 2003–2008, or by an announcement in the financial press and information systems such as Reuters.

Share suspension and liquidations

Shares listed on a stock exchange can be suspended for several reasons. In some cases it is because of a significant movement up or down in the share price and the exchange suspends the shares ahead of an announcement by the board, if they know the reason for the price volatility, or an announcement by, say, a bidding company of their intentions. In most cases the suspension is temporary and once the details of the relevant issues are in the public domain, the shares resume trading.

One serious reason for the suspension of the shares is if the company is experiencing financial difficulties such that it is to be placed into administration and possibly declared bankrupt or in liquidation. An investor in a company that goes into liquidation will be in the situation where the security is not only worthless but also un-negotiable. The security will be suspended in the relevant stock exchange(s) until such time as the liquidator is able to repay amounts due to the various classes of creditor. Once there is no more cash that can be retrieved for the creditors, the company is wound up and the certificates cancelled.

This process can take years to resolve and the global custodian must ensure that any information is passed to the client and that all expected liquidation payments are collected and paid to the client.

Proxy voting

It is obvious that with so much investment being cross-border there will be problems associated with the right of the shareholder to vote at company meetings and even to act on corporate actions. The main problem concerns time zones and delays in receiving the relevant information. For global custodians to act efficiently and effectively on behalf of their investing clients, timely information has to be received from the companies. It is necessary for the custodians to have highly skilled staff in order to decipher and translate lengthy technical information and then to organize it in such a way that the client can make a timely and informed decision on the options available.

To ensure that all clients' decisions are transmitted to the company, custodian banks' staff must:

- Be aware of the deadlines given by the company
- Inform the clients of these deadlines
- Ensure that missing client instructions are chased up before the deadline

■ Know the length of time it takes to send instructions to the company and in what format it can be sent and received

With the advent of widespread foreign share ownership there is clearly a demand for effective standards to be established covering, for instance:

■ Greater uniformity of information dissemination
■ Standardized timeframes
■ Reliable information databases with easy global access

These databases and the data communication networks connecting them to the information suppliers and users would be well suited to serve cross-border proxy voting.

This is an important issue as it is now universally accepted that all shareholders should have an opportunity to exercise their voting rights, even though many of them may not actually wish to cast their votes. Indeed, there are some countries which are now beginning to encourage a more proactive participation by shareholders in the affairs of the companies. As a result of increased shareholdings by large institutional investors, investment and pension fund managers have shown a new interest in exercising their voting rights. This is partly in response to expectations expressed by the various regulatory bodies and partly an apparent underlying desire to influence a company's business or information policy. For example, with adverse press comment on large bonuses being awarded to directors, sometimes when the company is apparently not performing partic- ularly well, both small and large shareholders are increasingly attending meetings and voicing concern.

Large cross-border investments are reinforcing this trend and the need for a mechanism that will permit the exercise of voting rights across borders with the same ease as is found in the investor's home country is very important. The rationalization in the industry with exchanges and clearing houses merging and greater regulatory harmony will go some way to achieving this. However, at present private investors rarely attend shareholders' meetings located overseas in person due to the distances and costs involved. In addition, the procedures surrounding shareholder voting vary greatly from country to country because there are different laws and traditions as well as the fact that there are different types of securities. By the very nature of some of the instruments companies do not always know the names of shareholders. The holders can only be contacted via the media or by custodians who research relevant information.

With registered shares the shareholders are advised by mail via the registrars and, if applicable, by the relevant nominee companies. However, we need to remember that in a number of countries there are equity-type instruments or shares which:

- Prohibit non-resident investors from voting
- Carry no voting rights (for example, preference shares – these will only carry voting rights if the company has failed to pay its preference dividend)
- Have a split voting structure (for example, companies can have both voting shares and non-voting, 'A', shares listed on the Stock Exchange)
- Where relevant documentation is published in a different language
- The issuer is domiciled in a different time zone causing huge problems in meeting formalities and requirements such as a printed proxy statement that must be completed and sent back to the agent

Thus we can see the dilemma facing both the custodian that offers a proxy voting service for international stocks and the client who often has very little time to organize a decision and subsequent instruction to the custodian.

Asset and cash management

While the custodians can offer various services linked to asset and cash management the client must be aware of the risks involved should a problem occur with the custodian. Part of the risk is a counterparty one, i.e. what happens if the custodian were to collapse? The other is, what is the alternative? Obviously the counterparty risk can be partially addressed by using suitably credit-rated organizations. The other is that there is a price to be paid in terms of requiring more sophisticated cash-monitoring systems and the extra expense associated with transferring cash around the banking system. The global custodians are aware of the problems involved and constantly seek new ways to keep the client's cash-related business in-house.

Single-currency accounts

Clients whose business generates cash predominantly in one currency and who wish to enter into cross-border trading might prefer to operate with cash accounts in a single currency. They will arrange for all purchase costs, sale proceeds and income receipts associated with the cross-border trades to be converted through a foreign exchange transaction into their base currency as and when the need arises or when there is a volatile situation with a currency that might create an unacceptable exchange rate risk. For the investor, the advantages are:

- The exposure to adverse foreign exchange rate movements is removed once the Forex trade has been executed.
- With only one currency, the funding requirement calculations are simplified.
- The investor is free to obtain the most advantageous exchange rates from the Forex marketplace.
- Cash reconciliation and control processes are more straightforward.

The possible disadvantages to be considered are:

- There will be extra Forex trading charges to consider over and above the securities trading commissions.
- The securities trade settlements will no longer be on a DVP basis as the currency movements will take place independently of the securities movements. The risk of non-performance of the trade as a whole is greater than it would be for a DVP settlement.
- For Forex trades dealt with counterparties other than the global custodian, the investor must give settlement instructions for the cash side in addition to instructions for the securities.

Global custodians will need to consider the implications of providing such as service and these implications will include:

- All income receipts are exchanged from time to time into the base currency and the custodian must be able to ensure that they have the capability. This must also be done as instructed and at a rate acceptable to the client that must be contained in the agreement.
- The global custodian, however, will not necessarily be responsible for exchanging the purchase and sale amounts as the investor will look around the foreign exchange market for the best foreign exchange rates.
- The global custodian will continue to settle trades in the relevant currency on a DVP basis (where applicable) and needs to be aware of the possible currency exposures this creates.
- The global custodian is not under an obligation to offer CSDA as the transfer of securities occurs independently from the movement of the client's cash.

Multi-currency accounts

Multi-currency banking will suit those clients whose ordinary business activities generate cash flows in foreign currencies and/or who prefer to settle the securities trades on a DVP basis in the foreign currency. The cash-funding requirements will be undertaken as a separate process. For the client, the advantages are:

- The securities trades benefit from DVP settlement
- The investor is able to take advantage of the global custodian's CSDA settlement service
- There are more options available in terms of subsequent use of the foreign currency balances.

The disadvantages are:

- The increased control and administrative burden as a result of operating many different currency accounts.

For the global custodian, the implications are:

- A more complete custody and banking service can be provided to the client.
- The need to exchange all income into the base currency is removed thus reducing the number of relatively small-value Forex trades that must be executed.

Interest-bearing accounts

In the financial markets the cost or value of money is always a critical factor. Effective use of cash contributes to the overall profits on trading and returns on investments. Any cash not being utilized to pay for purchases should be earning some kind of return. Often the amount of 'free' cash at any one point in time may be very large or very small and it may be available only for a short time. However, even if the cash is available for one day and is small in value it can earn interest. Over a year these individual and small interest amounts when combined become a more significant figure.

Therefore clients who actively manage their cash balances wish to reduce or eliminate the time that uninvested or uncommitted cash balances remain in non-interest-bearing accounts. Cash balances will be transferred to deposit accounts or other financial products. Although this achieves the objective, it increases the administrative burden and becomes expensive to operate. The global custodians now provide interest on various currency accounts and thus help to cut down the number of cash movements across the accounts.

Sweeping

The global custodian may offer to transfer automatically (or sweep) non-invested and uncommitted balances overnight from non-interest-bearing accounts into interest-bearing deposit accounts or other financial products that generate an interest return. This facility helps the treasury manager at the client to achieve a situation that ensures cash balances are being used in an efficient manner. Pooling is another facility that the custodian offers. Global custodians hold accounts in the same currency and/or multi-currency accounts for their clients. For interest calculations only the custodians can pool the balances by currency into one larger balance in order to attract a higher rate of interest or reduce the effect of some accounts being overdrawn.

Banking services

Global custodians are able to offer a wide range of banking services including:

- Funds transmission systems that enable the client to transfer electronically funds covering clean payments (i.e. those not directly connected to a securities trade).
- Treasury services that provide dealing facilities to purchase and sell foreign currency, place funds on deposit and draw down funds on loan.
- Screen-based dealing systems that some global custodians have now made available and which allow clients to execute their smaller Forex deals without reference to a bank dealer. Clients are

able to accept or reject the rates offered on the screen and, should the rate be acceptable, the transaction is immediately confirmed.

So the custodians can provide vital support in terms of the post-settlement activities on securities and the cash or treasury management process. They can also offer help in the areas of taxation and in the important area of reporting to clients.

Withholding tax (WHT)

Cash benefits paid by companies to their shareholders in the form of dividends are subject to withholding tax (WHT). WHT is deducted at source with the shareholder receiving the net amount. The tax authorities of the country where the company is based determine the rate of WHT that will apply. In some cases this may be zero, in others it is a significant rate.

With the increase in cross-border investment activity, investors are subject to different tax regimes. Tax reclaims must be made in the issuer's country of origin and these will be submitted by the global custodian on behalf of the client.

Double-taxation agreements

The problem for non-resident investors is that the net income is additionally subject to further taxation in their own country, i.e. the income is double-taxed. Most governments have recognized this issue as being unfair and allow most or all of the WHT to be reclaimed by entering into a double-taxation agreement (DTA) with other like-minded governments. Governments enter into DTAs with other countries in order to:

- Prevent income being taxed twice, and
- Render reciprocal assistance to prevent tax evasion.

WHT reclamation works along one of the following bases:

- Certain classes of income are made taxable only in one of the countries who are party to a DTA, e.g. in the country of the taxpayer's residence.
- Income is taxable in both countries but (in the case of UK residents) the overseas tax is allowable as a credit against UK tax.

As with most things to do with tax, the matter can be complex and the administrative burden in respect of WHT that the custodian takes on for the client is of real added-value

Investment accounting

Investment accounting is the provision of a full range of reports that may include fully accrued, multi-currency valuations, performance measurement, investment analysis, at both detailed and summary levels. Reports may apply to a single portfolio or a consolidation of a number of portfolios.

Pricing and valuation reporting

Prices of individual securities are obtained from a variety of external price feeds and allow the calculation of market value. From this the investors' portfolios can be valued in both the currency of the security and the base currency of the investor. It is important that the repricing of securities is carried out accurately and at timely intervals so funds' net asset value (NAV) calculations can be performed. An incorrectly priced security will lead to an erroneous NAV with the consequence that compensation might have to be paid to unit holders of the fund or funds concerned. A significant error may also need reporting to the trustees and the regulator.

Investment analysis

Analysing the investments is important in tracking the performance and return on the specific and collective holdings in the portfolios. Using pricing information, the investments can be analysed in a variety of ways:

- By instrument type – equities (ordinary/common shares, preference shares, etc.), bonds (Eurobonds, government bonds, convertible bonds, etc.) and cash and cash equivalents
- By industrial sector
- By geographical location
- Percentage of the portfolio that each security or its type, industrial sector and geographical location represents
- 'What-if' analysis by examining how changes in securities or country allocations affect the return on the portfolio.

The performance of investments is also made against a benchmark such as an index.

Investment performance evaluation

The information provided allows the investor to evaluate the marketability of the securities by stock selection, markets and currencies. There are a number of external performance measurement companies who collect relevant data from investors or global custodians in order to determine how investor types compare with each other or against industry-recognized indices. This is relevant, for example, for marketing purposes when fund managers hoping to win new business will state that they have outperformed the relevant index by, say, 2% when the average has been 1%.

Investment income tracking

The investment performance of a security includes the income received and income due. This is especially important for debt securities for which income (interest) accrues on a daily basis until the payment is made (usually annually or bi-annually depending on the security type and domicile).

Foreign exchange reporting

Foreign exchange transactions should be related back to the underlying securities trades or income receipts. Historical exchange rates and interest rates should be reported to allow the investor to check the actual rates obtained against the market closing rates. As we noted earlier, custodians offer a variety of services related to currency management and Forex dealing and making comparisons for competitiveness are essential.

Consolidated reporting

Investors might use two or more fund managers, because each has a particular specialist investment skill. If the fund managers use their own global custodian, the investors have the problem of consolidating a range of reports from the fund managers and their global custodians into one combined set of reports.

To save the investors time and effort in making the consolidation, one global custodian acts as recipient for the reports generated by the other global custodians and prepares the consolidated set of reports.

We have seen in this chapter the extensive role and services that the custodians offer to their clients. The challenge for the custodians is twofold. First, can they keep pace with the changes in the marketplace and the ever-increasing demands from the clients for new and innovative support services? The second is to be aware of the threats and opportunities the rationalization of the markets offers.

Today the international CSDs are providing almost an identical range of services that the custodian offers. There is a significant use of services offered by large banks like prime brokerage and these are still being developed and incorporating new services and products, some of which compete with those offered by custodians. The future for custodians is very much about moving with the times, meeting the challenges and developing the opportunities that the changes are offering.

Chapter 7

Other clearing and settlement

In the previous chapters we have looked at the clearing and settlement of bonds, equities and derivatives. We have also considered the role of the clearing house and custodians and settlement processes related to corporate actions and cash/asset management. We can look at some of the more specific products and services and also at what else might fall into the category of clearing, settlement and custody.

RepoClear

In August 1999, London Clearing House (LCH) introduced LCH RepoClear, the first multi-market centralized clearing and netting facility for the European government repo and cash bond (outright) market. Today, LCH RepoClear currently clears Austrian, Belgian, Dutch and German government bonds and German Jumbo Pfandbriefe repos and cash bonds and other European government bond repo and cash bond markets will be added in the future.

There were good reasons why LCH considered introducing the RepoClear product. Banks active in the European repo markets were experiencing difficulties in maintaining and, indeed, increasing their repo activities as they ran into internal balance sheet, capital and credit limit constraints. To overcome these LCH and a group of banks that were already members of LCH embarked on a project to develop a repo clearing and netting facility. After carrying out a feasibility study among its members, LCH began work in earnest, liaising closely with the leading repo banks in Europe to develop the RepoClear service.

After a successful launch in October 1999, LCH agreed to join with Euroclear and the Government Securities Clearing Corporation (GSCC) in the USA to continue the development of LCH RepoClear on a joint basis. The three parties have formed the European Securities Clearing Corporation (ESCC) to guide the further development of LCH RepoClear.

In common with the other clearing services it provides, LCH adopts a settlement and payment netting and margin processes in RepoClear.

Settlement netting

At a prescribed time per individual market, LCH nets all delivery obligations (i.e. start leg, end leg and substitutions) due for settlement the next business day. The ideal result is for one net delivery obligation to be calculated. (In certain markets, the settlement netting may result in several delivery obligations due to cross-border settlement or maximum delivery size requirements.) There are two methods for the delivery of information to the appropriate depositories. LCH can inform members of their delivery obligations with the members then sending instructions to the depositories or, if the member has signed a Power of Attorney agreement, LCH can send the member's delivery instructions directly to the depository.

Payment netting

If, after the settlement netting cycle, there are no securities delivery obligations (longs equal shorts), LCH aggregates all net cash delivery obligations into one amount per market, which is paid through the appropriate depository. Coupon payments are netted with other cash flows in each currency and reduced to one cash flow per currency per day. Margin and settlement amounts from a member's other LCH activities are netted, resulting in a single payment or receipt, per currency per day.

Margin

In the course of daily operations, LCH nets all margin obligations from all exchange-traded and bilaterally traded contracts, together with any coupon payments, into a single payment per currency per day, paid through the Protected Payments System (PPS). Using current market prices, LCH recalculates the net present value (NPV) of members' repo positions at the close of each business day. NPV is the value of the bond leg amount (collateral) less the value of the cash leg. The change in members' NPV (today's NPV minus yesterday's) is its variation margin which is paid and received each day, in cash per currency, through the PPS. The use of cash to pay variation margin is due to settlement system considerations.

LCH requires members to post initial margin to protect it against the possible losses incurred in the time it would take to close out a defaulting member's portfolio. Throughout the day, LCH monitors the impact of changing prices and positions on the value of members' portfolios and associated initial margin requirements. If the protection afforded by the initial margin has been significantly eroded by price movements, or the initial margin requirement has significantly increased, LCH will make intra-day margin calls. LCH accepts the same range of collateral (including cash, bank guarantees or letters of credit, certain government bonds and certain equities) for initial margin as for its other business.

Futures and options centralized clearing

In the exchange-traded derivatives markets the use of centralized clearing services is common. Banks and brokers offer their clients the ability to have their transactions executed by counterparties of their choice but the settlement process is centralized through one counterparty. It can be easily defined as:

> **The channelling of clearing and settlement of all futures and options transactions through a single counterparty**

Called centralized or global clearing it offers advantages and disadvantages to both the broker/bank offering the service and the client utilizing it. The advantages and disadvantages for **the broker** are:

Advantages	Disadvantages
Additional revenue generated from an operations function	Operations assume greater risk than that generated by the in-house principal and client activity
Fully utilizes the systems and resource that is needed anyway for principal business	Can create much greater volumes and therefore costs
Can reduce margin needed at the clearing house through the effect of netted positions	Requires careful management of deadlines and procedures to avoid errors
Can be offered as part of a prime brokerage package	Requires efficient, and reliable system(s) with capability to handle different products

The advantages and disadvantages for **the client** are:

Advantages	Disadvantages
Single relationship for settlement activity	Counterparty risk concentrated with one clearer
Efficient use of margin offset and collateral	Confidentiality worries on sensitive position and trading data

Advantages	**Disadvantages**
One source of information on positions etc	Can become 'locked in' to the technology services offered making a change of broker difficult
More efficient reporting and risk management	
Less administration and reduced costs	
Can better utilize technology and other added-value services provided by the clearer	

The flows associated with centralized derivative clearing can be illustrated by Figure 7.1. The client places orders with different brokers who will execute the trades on the exchange. The trades are then rerouted at the clearing house into the account of the global clearer.

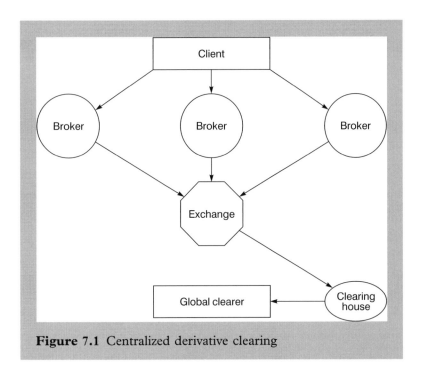

Figure 7.1 Centralized derivative clearing

The global clearer will now settle the trades with the clearing house and the client. As part of the service the brokerage due to the execution brokers is paid by the clearer who in turn includes this amount in their clearing charge to the client.

Treasury operations

The treasury function is primarily concerned with money in terms of cash management, transmission and receipt of funds and controlling the risk associated with these processes. In Chapter 6 we saw how custodians are very much involved in this process with their clients.

Treasury settlement is in effect the support function for the activity of dealers in cash instruments as well as providing cash management for other areas of the business using (borrowing) money or depositing excess funds. This activity will naturally include foreign exchange transactions. Generically the treasury settlement function is similar to that for the securities we have already looked at in the book. So we have deal capture, deal verification and settlement instructions. Key elements of the process are dates and rates, as well as confirms.

Money we know is based on value dates and the rate, cost or return available or due on that money. Confirms related to the deals and the settlement therefore incorporate reconciliation of amounts or value and the value date. Confirmations and instructions are often part of straightthrough processing (STP) used by many banks in treasury settlement. Settlement takes place by either netting or real-time gross settlement (RTGS).

Payments are the end-product of the treasury settlement process. Naturally payment systems are geared towards the type and frequency of the movements of cash. There are retail funds transfer systems that cater for high-volume/low-value and cover market sectors like cheques, credit card payments and cash machines. Large value funds transfer systems are used in the wholesale cash markets and examples of such systems are:

- Clearing House Interbank Payment System (CHIPS) in the USA
- Clearing House Automated Payment System (CHAPS) in the UK
- Trans-European Automated Real-Time Gross Settlement Express Transfer (TARGET) which links RTGS national payment systems in Europe for the euro

Payment instructions are sent via SWIFT messages or if the organization is a direct member by one of the domestic high-value payment systems. An alternative way of sending instructions is via telex or a proprietary electronic link operated by the correspondent bank (the agent appointed by an organization to manage the international payment and receipt of funds).

One significant issue for treasury settlement teams is the potential for risk caused by errors in instructions, missing deadlines, authorizing payments without reconciling the confirms, etc. Reconciliation of the cash movements in and out of the correspondent or nostro bank accounts is crucially important.

Continuous linked settlement (CLS)

In foreign exchange markets cash payments have been made as part of the treasury function. One possible risk with this has been the chance that because of time zones a payment in one currency could be made from one bank to another with a corresponding payment in a different currency going the other way a few hours later.

If before the second currency moved the paying bank should default the other bank would not only lose the currency it has already paid but also would not receive the second currency. Just such a situation occurred with a German bank, ID Herstatt, in 1974 that received Deutsche Marks in Frankfurt but collapsed before the dollar side of the transaction settled in New York.

Since then netting has been looked upon as a way of removing some elements of the risk in foreign exchange settlement.

More recently the CLS Bank has considered providing a form of clearing for FX settlement not unlike the facility offered by LCH and other central counterparties. The CLS Bank will transfer funds electronically between members, accounts at the due time of settlement and take margin collateral to ensure that the money moves physically in the relevant time zone. This will enable parties to FX trades to be confident that settlement risk has then been removed.

Readers may like to note that the whole subject of controls and risk is covered in another book in this series.

Chapter 8

Operational issues and the future

In the book so far we have looked at the key issues surrounding equity, debt, derivatives and custody. By now the reader will be aware that clearing, settlement and custody are not small operational processes. Also the reader will be aware that the whole financial markets process is totally dependent on the efficient, accurate and cost-effective operations process.

In another book in this series we describe controls and procedures and clearly these play a significant role in the clearing and settlement processes. For the operations manager and the team the objectives are to devise procedures and processes that result in an effective and efficient settlement process. What issues will arise in pursuit of this goal?

There are likely to be many and they will differ from one organization to another. Key issues are described below.

Direct or indirect clearing membership

Direct membership of the clearing house will create a different criterion for the processes and procedures to be undertaken by the operations team. As a clearing member there are the clearing house rules and regulations to consider and comply with. There will be timings and deadlines for instructions, payments, delivery etc., depending on the market being used. In the case of a CCP there will be legally binding obligations that will apply, for example, with any futures contracts positions and with the establishing of guaranteed payment facilities like the Protected Payment System operated by LCH. This system requires an account to be opened by the clearing member at a bank designated as approved by LCH from which the clearing house can call amounts for settlement of obligations at a prescribed time each day.

Apart from understanding the procedures for clearing and settlement that apply to the particular clearing house, the need to effectively segregate principal and client positions and assets is a crucial regulatory requirement.

There is also the issue of managing the relationship with any non-clearing members and clients. The clearing member of the CCP is, as we have just said, liable to the CCP for all the transactions held in its name. Any delay in settlement by the client and the clearing member must either settle on the client's behalf, i.e. incur funding and asset management requirements, claim costs from client, etc., or close the position.

There are advantages to being a clearing member but there are equally disciplines and resourcing issues that the operations teams and managers face.

Resources

People, processes and systems – the operations team obviously needs certain levels of resources to be able to manage the clearing and settlement function. In the previous chapters we have looked at the characteristics of the products, the pre- and post-settlement events and the ongoing issues of safekeeping and custody. Paramount in terms of resource management are the systems and the skills sets or the people.

Neither is a particularly straightforward issue for the operations manager. In today's financial markets the diversity of instruments traded and the strategies utilized means that the organization must be structured not so much along specific product lines, as has often been the case in the past, but rather as a flexible, multi-product-based unit. Among the key issues to be addressed are:

- Product knowledge
- Systems capabilities and reliability
- Data management
- Information sources
- Information distribution
- Risk awareness
- Workflow management
- Client services
- Personnel development
- Business development
- Change management

These headings are not in any particular order of importance and their impact will vary from one organization to another. However, all of them will certainly be an issue for the operations manager at some stage and relating them to the current and future clearing and settlement processes is going to be crucial to the success of the business.

Clearing and settlement objectives

If the management of people and systems is a key function of the managers and supervisors then the clearing and settlement objectives need to be established. The objectives might be summarized as:

- Ensure compliance with department and group-wide risk management policies
- Set and maintain high levels of efficiency

- Ensure the operations function is cost effective
- Identify and develop policies and practices to gain and maintain competitive advantage
- Develop and implement procedures to provide a secure and effective operation
- Control the workflow
- Ensure compliance with regulation and controls
- Establish an ongoing business development programme for the operations function
- Create a continuity programme and development schedule for staff
- Provide high quality client services
- Maintain efficient and accurate record keeping

The demands on managers and supervisors are considerable if the above are to be achieved. Today the role has been further expanded and as well as operational issues such as processes and procedures, we now have greater skills requirements in the client-facing and risk-management areas. We can also add to this an involvement in profit generation and protection as many operations teams move from 'service and support' functions to 'revenue' functions.

Disaster recovery

All businesses need disaster recovery policies. Operations central to the businesses in the financial markets must be able to continue to operate or the consequence would be to curtail or even stop trading activity. As this can only be a last-resort option there needs to be in place adequate procedures and contingencies to ensure the critical operations functions will continue.

Externally, clearing houses and custodians will have their contingency plans for partial or full interruption to the function and internally the operations team will be part of the group-wide contingency plans.

However, it is not always the wholesale disruption caused by, say, a building fire that causes the most impact. The reason is fairly obvious in that any firm has full-scale disaster recovery plans. What causes more problem is the intermittent but significant interruption to business created by, for example, system downs, excess (to capacity) workflow or communication problems.

This issue is overcome by having clear procedures, including escalation of action requirements, short-term support contingencies and flexible procedures that are introduced when the standard procedure cannot be followed. The issue of controls, procedures and risk is a very large subject and is covered in greater detail in another book in this series.

The future and managing change

We have frequently referred in this book to the change taking place in the industry and managing that change is a very real challenge. Probably the hardest part is the development and implementation of enhanced and new systems to deal with STP, the central clearing counterparty process, globalized clearing, etc. The shortening settlement cycles in equity settlement, greater use of collateral as margin becomes more central in the settlement processes and the use of netting across different products all require changes to systems, procedures and processes.

The need to develop innovative client services is also a pressure that the operations have acquired and the increasing emphasis on operations and operational risk management is changing the role of operations and the operations manager forever.

An effective, efficient and risk-managed operations function is no longer a nice to have but is instead a critically important requirement for the business. Clearing and settlement is no longer an administrative process but is a function that can make or break a business.

As change and competitiveness issues increase so does the pressure to meet the challenge. Not all firms, despite their outward posturing, have the ability or even the desire to meet that challenge. For them there will be a missed opportunity, for those that do meet the challenge the rewards may be very significant indeed.

To use a frequently quoted term – 'Watch this space!'

Appendix 1

Relevant websites

www.afma.com	Australian Financial Markets Association
www.asx.com.au	Australian Stock Exchange
www.bis.org	Bank for International Settlement
www.cbl-ltd.co.uk	Computer Based Learning Ltd
www.cboe.com	Chicago Board Options Exchange
www.cbot.com	Chicago Board of Trade
www.cftc.gov	Commodities Future Trading Commission
www.clearnetsa.com	
www.clearstream.com	
www.cme.com	Chicago Mercantile Exchange
www.crestco.co.uk	
www.dtc.org	Depository Trust Company
www.ecsda.com	European Central Securities Depositories Association
www.eurexchange.com	
www.euroclear.com	
www.foa.co.uk	Futures and Options Association
www.fiafii.org	Futures Industry Association
www.fsa.go.jp	Financial Services Agency Japan

www.fsa.gov.uk	Financial Services Authority
www.hkex.com.hk	Hong Kong Exchanges and Clearing
www.isma.co.uk	International Securities Markets Association
www.issanet.org	International Securities Services Association
www.lch.co.uk	London Clearing House
www.liffe.com	London International Financial Futures & Options Exchange
www.lme.co.uk	London Metal Exchange
www.londonstockexchange.com	
www.nasdaq.com	
www.norex.com	Norex Alliance
www.nyse.com	New York Stock Exchange
http://risk.ifci.ch/	G30 Recommendations
www.sec.gov	Securities Exchange Commission (US)
www.ses.com.sg	Singapore Exchange
www.tse.or.jp	Tokyo Stock Exchange
www.virtx.com	

Appendix 2

Understanding London SPAN

The primary role of LCH is to act as central counterparty to trades executed by its members:

- In futures and options contracts on the London International Financial Futures and Options Exchange (LIFFE), the London Metal Exchange (LME) and the International Petroleum Exchange (IPE)
- In certain classes of over-the-counter (OTC) products, specifically interbank interest rate swaps, repos and cash bonds
- For equities traded on the London Stock Exchange's SETS system
- OTC energy swaps transacted on the Intercontinental Exchange announced 29 August 2001
- In 2000 LCH cleared approximately 224 million contracts traded on the London exchanges.

When LCH has registered a trade, it becomes the buyer to every LCH member who sells and the seller to every LCH member who buys, ensuring the financial performance of trades. To protect itself against the risks assumed as central counterparty, LCH establishes the margin requirements as described below.

What is margining?

As central counterparty to its members' trades, LCH is at risk from the default of a member. To limit and cover such potential loss, LCH collects margin on all open positions and recalculates members' margin liabilities on a daily basis. There are two major types:

- Initial margin
- Variation margin

Initial margin is the deposit required on all net positions and is returned by LCH to members when positions are closed. Members may impose more stringent initial margin requirements on their own customers, in accordance with the rules of the relevant exchanges.

Variation margin is members' profits or losses which are calculated daily from the market-to-market close value of their open position. These amounts, depending on individual contract terms, are either realized – that is, credited to or debited from member accounts – or treated as unrealized profits or losses.

Realized variation margin

Many contracts are subject to daily variation margin payments and receipts. For example, a member buys 10 December FT-SE 100 index futures at 5100 points and later sells at 5110 points. The contract size is £10 per index point. Given the daily price moves shown below, the variation margin payments to (CR) and receipts from (DR) the member during the life of the open position would be as follows.

Day	Trade price	Net position	Closing price	Price movement	Variation margin (£)	Cumulative variation
1	5100	+10	5110	+10	1000CR	1000CR
2		+10	5140	+30	3000CR	4000CR
3		+10	5120	−20	2000CR	2000CR
4	5100	0		−10	1000DR	1000CR

Total variation margin over duration of position   **1000CR**

The difference between the future's price (5100 points) and the price at which the trade was closed (5110 points) represents a net profit of 10 points, so a total variation margin receipt of £1000 (net profit [10 points] *no of lots [10]) will have been credited to the member over the duration of the position.

Discount variation margin

For the London Metal Exchange's (LME) contracts profit or loss is not immediately realized but becomes due on the prompt date of the contract. Its value is therefore not its absolute amount, but the amount discounted by the interest return which would be made if the money were immediately available.

Thus, for a contract (e.g. CAD) forwards variation margin for a given trade for a given prompt date is calculated as:

$$VM = (\text{closing price} - \text{trades price}) \times \text{net position}$$

The values at prompt date level are discounted to present value by multiplying by a discount factor for that prompt date. The discounted variation margins for each of the prompt dates in the portfolio are summed to give a single discounted forwards variation margin figure for that contract which could be positive or negative.

Net liquidating value

Net liquidating value is calculated on all premium paid up front options. For example, a member sells a December Boots option contract for a premium of £0.10 a share (1 contract = 1000 shares). Given the daily price movements shown below, unrealized variation margin during the life of the position is as follows.

Credit net liquidating values can be used to offset other liabilities. Debit net liquidating values must be paid.

Day	Trade price	Closing price	Net liquidating value (£)	Premium payment (£)
1	0.10	0.10	100DR	100CR
2		0.09	90DR	
3		0.11	110DR	
4		0.08	80DR	
5	0.08	0.08		80DR

Delivery margin

Delivery margin is calculated on all deliverable contracts. For example, when an options contract is exercised it becomes a contract to deliver ('delivery contract') the underlying shares. The delivery of shares is effected via LCH and is made on a rolling settlement basis. LCH is exposed to the risk of changes in the underlying share value during the period the delivery contract is awaiting settlement. During this period initial margin will continue to be calculated using London SPAN. In addition, a contingent variation margin is calculated as the difference between the strike price of the option and the underlying share price which may be a credit or debit.

For example, a member exercises 1 call option on Boots with a strike price of £2.10 (1 contract = 1000 shares). Given the daily prices shown below the contingent variation margin during the delivery cycle is as follows.

Day	Underlying price (£)	Strike price (£)	Contingent variation margin
1	2.20	2.10	100CR
2	2.18	2.10	80CR
3	2.21	2.10	110CR

Initial margin

LCH uses London SPAN to calculate initial margin requirements for IPE, LIFFE and LME. London SPAN builds on and adapts the SPAN (Standard Portfolio Analysis of Risk) framework developed by the Chicago Mercantile Exchange.[1]

Inputs to London SPAN

There are three major inputs to the London SPAN margin calculation – Positions, Prices and Parameters – sometimes referred to as the three Ps. A change to any one of these will result in a change to the margin requirement.

Initial margin parameters

LCH sets initial margin parameters for each contract in conjunction with the exchanges. These are potential market moves for which LCH requires margin cover. The two main parameters are a futures price move – either known as the initial margin rate or the futures scanning range – and an implied volatility shift relevant to options contracts. These are set with reference to historical data on prices and volatilities and other factors such as known forthcoming price-sensitive events. The parameters are kept under continuous review by LCH but do not change on a daily basis. They are inputs to London SPAN.

How does London SPAN calculate initial margins?

London SPAN divides contracts into groups of futures and options relating to a single underlying asset (e.g. coffee futures and options on coffee futures). In this note these groups will subsequently be referred to as 'portfolios'. At the first stage of calculation, London

[1] The CME permitted LCH to adapt the CME version of SPAN to produce the London version of SPAN. The CME assumes no liability in connection with the use of London SPAN or the London version of PC-SPAN.

SPAN simulates how the value of a 'portfolio' would react to the changing market conditions defined in the initial margin parameters. This is done by adopting a series of market scenarios and evaluating the 'portfolio' under these conditions.

For example, the futures scanning range for the LIFFE coffee contract is $50/tonne and the volatility shift parameter is 10%. The closing price of coffee is $1275/tonne and the implied volatility is 25%.

In this case, London SPAN uses sixteen scenarios consisting of implied volatilities increasing or decreasing by 2.5% (i.e. 10% of 25%), and futures prices increasing or decreasing by proportions of the futures scanning range (see below).

Futures	Implied volatility changes	Futures price ($/tonne)	Implied volatility (%)
Futures price down 3/3 range	volatility up	1225	27.5
Futures price down 3/3 range	volatility down	1225	22.5
Futures price down 2/3 range	volatility up	1242	27.5
Futures price down 2/3 range	volatility down	1242	22.5
Futures price down 1/3 range	volatility up	1258	27.5
Futures price down 1/3 range	volatility down	1258	22.5
Futures price unchanged	volatility up	1275	27.5
Futures price unchanged	volatility down	1275	22.5
Futures price up 1/3 range	volatility up	1292	27.5
Futures price up 1/3 range	volatility down	1292	22.5
Futures price up 2/3 range	volatility up	1308	27.5
Futures price up 2/3 range	volatility down	1308	22.5
Futures price up 3/3 range	volatility up	1325	27.5
Futures price up 3/3 range	volatility down	1325	22.5
Futures up extreme move	volatility unchanged	1375	25.0
Futures down extreme move	volatility unchanged	1375	25.0

The last two scenarios use a move of twice the normal futures scanning range but only 35% of the value is used. They evaluate the risk of deep out-of-the money options, which may not otherwise be assessed.

Having defined the scenarios, London SPAN then evaluates the potential profits/losses for each contract (futures month or option series) by comparing the current price with the calculated contract price for each scenario. Option prices are estimated using an appropriate option pricing model for the contract. The sixteen profits/losses for each contract form a risk array. A risk array is calculated for each futures delivery month and options series.

Risk arrays are calculated each day using the closing futures and options prices.

Scanning risk

By valuing each net position (future or option) with the appropriate array and then combining the arrays, London SPAN determines which is the worst loss scenario for the 'portfolio'. This is referred to as the scanning risk.

Inter-month spread charge

When calculating the scanning risk, London SPAN initially assumes that futures prices move by exactly the same amount across all contracts months; therefore, a long position in one month exactly offsets a short position in another month.

Since futures prices do not correlate exactly across contract months, gains in one month may not exactly offset losses in another and vice versa. Therefore, 'portfolios' face inter-month price risk. London SPAN calculates an inter-month spread charge to cover this risk by netting the position across different months, using the delta value of options to convert them to equivalent futures.

Strategy spreads

As a first step towards calculating inter-month spread charges, for specific contracts SPAN will look for particular strategy positions (e.g. condors and butterflys) and apply an appropriate charge to these.

Multi-tier inter-month spreads

SPAN uses a multi-tier inter-month spread method which allows different spread rates to be set within and between specified groups of expiries. In its most simple form (which is applied to a large number of contracts) a single tier will be defined which covers all expiries.

Spot month charge

Volatility can increase when a contract approaches the last day of trading or the day of delivery of the underlying. LCH covers this risk by building an additional spot month charge into London SPAN.

Inter-commodity spread credit

In certain cases, offsets or margin liabilities in respect of different contracts are allowed across 'portfolios'. The inter-commodity spread credits recognize cases where offsetting positions in price-related but discrete contracts reduce overall portfolio risk. The offset reduces the amount of margin required on the spread position. Details of spreads allowed are available from LCH's Risk department or from frequently distributed LCH and exchange circulars.

LCH and the exchanges decide where it is justifiable, on risk assessment criteria, to allow inter-contract margin offsets and set the corresponding spread credit rates. Delta spreads are calculated and then used with these parameters to calculate the inter-commodity spread credits. The calculation of inter-commodity spread credits is explained in detail in the London SPAN Technical Information Package (TIP).

Inter-Commodity Spread Credit =
weighted futures price risk × spread credit
rate × no. of spreads × delta spread ratio

Total initial margin calculation

At the final stage, London SPAN brings together the various charges and the inter-commodity spread credit to provide a total initial margin requirement for the member's open positions:

London SPAN total initial margin =
scanning risk + inter-month spread charge +
spot month charge – inter-commodity spread credit

Short option minimum charge

Certain option portfolios may show zero or minimal risk when assessed using the standard London SPAN scenarios (volatility and futures scanning range). In these cases, London SPAN requires a minimum charge for each net short option. The charge sets an absolute minimum margin for the portfolio. If the short option minimum charge is lower than the total initial margin calculated, it is ignored:

Short option minimum charge =
net short position × short option minimum charge

How do I calculate a London SPAN margin?

London SPAN margins can be calculated in members' or clients' offices. A member may, however, charge a greater initial margin to its clients than LCH requires from its members. You will need to receive risk parameter files supplied by LCH. These should be loaded into your system and applied to your positions to calculate London SPAN initial margins. This can be done by programming the London SPAN calculations into your system, or by using PC London SPAN, a specially designed PC software program.

PC London SPAN generates a series of reports which show the breakdown of the London SPAN initial margin calculations. The following examples illustrate some simple London SPAN margin calculations.

For a simple futures position initial margin is calculated as the net position multiplied by initial margin rate.

- Net position = long 10 September FTSE futures
- scanning range = £3000 per lot
- initial margin = 10 × 3000 = £30 000

For a contract where a single inter-month spread charge rate applies, the spread margin required is calculated as the number of spreads multiplied by the inter-month spread charge:

- Position = long 10 September FTSE futures short 5 December FTSE futures
- No. of spreads = 5

Contract	Position	Dn 3/3 Vol up/dn	Dn 2/3 Vol up/dn	Dn 1/3 Vol up/dn	No change	Up 1/3 Vol up/dn	Up 2/3 Vol up/dn	Up 3/3 Vol up/dn
Sep FTSE	+10	+3000	+2000	+1000	0	−1000	−2000	−3000
		+3000	+2000	+1000	0	−1000	−2000	−3000
Dec FTSE	−5	+1500	−1000	−500	0	+500	+1000	+1500
		+1500	−1000	−500	0	+500	+1000	+1500
Total	+5	+1500	+1000	+500	0	−500	−1000	1500
		+1500	+1000	+500	0	−500	−1000	−1500

- Inter-month spread charge rate = £60
- Inter-month spread charge = 5 × 60 = £300

The total margin in the above example would be calculated as the sum of the scanning risk and the inter-month spread charge.

Scanning risks will be the maximum loss. It should be noted that on SPAN reports losses are usually shown as a positive number.

The largest loss is £1500 and occurs at the price down 3/3 scenario. It should be noted that as these are futures-only positions, adjusting the volatility has no impact. The theoretical losses for the volatility up and volatility down scenarios are the same.

We already know that the inter-month spread charge is £300. Therefore

$$\text{Total initial margin} = £1500 + £300$$
$$= £1800$$

Glossary

30/360 Also 360/360 or 30(E)/360. A day/year count convention assuming 30 days in each calendar month and a 'year' of 360 days; adjusted in America for certain periods ending on 31st-day of the month (and then sometimes known as 30(A)/360).

AAA The highest credit rating for a company or asset – the risk of default is negligible.

Accrued interest Interest due on a bond or other fixed income security that must be paid by the buyer of a security to its seller. Usual compensation: coupon rate of interest times elapsed days from prior interest payment date (i.e. coupon date) up to but not including settlement date.

Actual settlement date Date the transaction effectively settles in the clearing house (exchange of securities eventually against cash).

Add-on In capital adequacy calculations, the extra capital required to allow for the possibility of a deal moving into profit before a mark-to-market calculation is next made.

Affirmation Affirmation refers to the counterparty's agreement with the terms of the trade as communicated.

Agent One who executes orders for or otherwise acts on behalf of another (the principal) and is subject to its control and authority. The agent takes no financial risk and may receive a fee or commission.

Agent bank A commercial bank that provides services as per their instructions.

Allocation (give up) The process of moving the trade from the executing broker to the clearing broker in exchange-traded derivatives.

Amortization   Accounting procedure that gradually reduces the cost value of a limited life asset or intangible asset through periodic charges to income. The purpose of amortization is to reflect the resale or redemption value. Amortization also refers to the reduction of debt by regular payments of interest and principal to pay off a loan by maturity.

Annuity   For the recipient, an arrangement whereby the individual receives a pre-specified payment annually for a pre-specified number of years.

Ask price   Price at which a market-maker will sell stock. Also known as the offer price.

Assets   Everything of value that is owned or is due: fixed assets (cash, buildings and machinery) and intangible assets (patents and goodwill).

Assignment   The process by which the holder of a short option position is matched against a holder of a similar long option position who has exercised his right.

Authentication agent   A bank putting a signature on each physical bond to certify its genuineness prior to the distribution of the definitive bonds on the market.

Bank of England   The UK's central bank which undertakes policy decided by the Treasury and determines interest rates.

Bankers' acceptance   Short-term negotiable discount note, drawn on and accepted by banks which are obliged to pay the face value amount at maturity.

Bargain   Another word for a transaction or deal. It does not imply that a particularly favourable price was obtained.

Base currency   Currency chosen for reporting purposes.

Basis (gross)   The difference between the relevant cash instrument price and the futures price. Often used in the context of hedging the cash instrument.

Basis (value or net)   The difference between the gross basis and the carry.

Basis point (BP)   A change in the interest rate of one hundredth of one per cent (0.01%). One basis point is written as 0.01 when 1.0 represents 1%.

Basis risk   The risk that the price or rate of one instrument or position might not move exactly in line with the price or rate of another instrument or position which is being used to hedge it.

BBA   British Bankers' Association.

Bear   Investor who believes prices will fall.

Bearer document   Documents which state on them that the person in physical possession (the bearer) is the owner.

Benchmark bond   The most recently issued and most liquid government bond.

Beneficial owner   The underlying owner of a security who has paid for the stock and is entitled to the benefits of ownership.

Bid   (a) The price or yield at which a purchaser is willing to buy a given security. (b) To quote a price or yield at which a purchaser is able to buy a given security.

Bilateral netting   A netting system in which all trades executed on the same date in the same security between the same counter-parties are grouped and netted to one final delivery versus payment.

Bill of exchange   A money market instrument.

BIS   Bank for International Settlements.

Block trade   A purchase or sale of a large number of shares or dollar value of bonds normally much more than what constitutes a round lot in the market in question.

Bond   A certificate of debt, generally long-term, under the terms of which an issuer contracts, *inter alia*, to pay the holder a fixed principal amount on a stated future date and, usually, a series of interest payments during its life.

Bonus issue   A free issue of shares to a company's existing shareholders. No money changes hands and the share price falls pro rata. It is a cosmetic exercise to make the shares more marketable. Also known as a capitalization or scrip issue.

Book entry transfer   System of recording ownership of securities by computer where the owners do not receive a certificate. Records are kept (and altered) centrally in 'the book'.

Books closed day   Last date for the registration of shares or bonds for the payment of the next.

Break   A term used for any out-of-balance condition. A money break means that debits and credits are not equal. A trade break means that some information such as that from a contra broker is missing to complete that trade.

Broker/dealer   Any member firm of the Stock Exchange except the specialists which are GEMMs and IDBs.

Broken date   A maturity date other than the standard ones normally quoted.

Broken period   A period other than the standard ones normally quoted.

Broking   The activity of representing a client as agent and charging commission for doing so.

Bull   Investor who believes prices will rise.

Buying in   The action taken by a broker failing to receive delivery of securities from a counterparty on settlement date to purchase these securities in the open market.

Call deposits   Deposits which can be called (or withdrawn) at the option of the lender (and in some cases the borrower) after a specified period. The period is short, usually one or two days, and interest is paid at prevailing short-term rates (call account).

Call option   An option that gives the seller the right, but not the obligation, to buy a specified quantity of the underlying asset at a fixed price, on or before a specified date. The buyer of a call option has the obligation (because they have bought the right) to make delivery of the underlying asset if the option is exercised by the seller.

Callable bond   A bond that the issuer has the right to redeem prior to maturity by paying some specified call price.

Capital adequacy   Requirement for firms conducting investment business to have sufficient funds.

Capital markets   A term used to describe the means by which large amounts of money (capital) are raised by companies, governments and other organizations for long-term use and the subsequent trading of the instruments issued in recognition of such capital.

Capitalization issue   *See* **Bonus issues**.

CASCADE   Name of the settlement system used by Clearstream for German equity settlement.

Cash market   A term used to describe the market where the cash asset trades, or the underlying market when talking about derivatives.

Cash sale   A transaction on the floor of the stock exchange which calls for delivery of the securities that same day. In 'regular way' trades, the seller delivers securities on the fifth business day.

Cash settlement   In the money market a transaction is said to be made for cash settlement if the securities purchased are delivered against payment on the same day the trade is made.

Central securities depository   An organization which holds securities in either immobilized or dematerialized form thereby enabling transactions to be processed by book entry transfer. Also provides securities administration services.

Certificate of deposit   A money market instrument.

CFTC   The Commodities and Futures Commission, (United States).

Chaps   Clearing House Automated Payment System – clearing system for sterling and Euro payments between banks.

Cheapest to deliver   The cash security that provides the lowest cost (largest profit) to the arbitrage trader; the cheapest to deliver instrument is used to price the futures contract.

Clean price   The total price of a bond less accrued interest.

Clearance   The process of determining accountability for the exchange of money and securities between counterparties to a trade: clearance creates statements of obligation for securities and/or funds due.

Clearance broker   A broker who will handle the settlement of securities related transactions for himself or another broker. Sometimes small brokerage firms may not clear for themselves and therefore employ the services of an outside clearing broker.

Clearing   The centralized process whereby transacted business is recorded and positions are maintained.

Clearing house   Company that acts as central counterparty for the settlement of stock exchange transactions. For example, on TD,

Broker X sold 100, 300 and 500 securities ABC and purchased 50 and 200 units of the same issue. The clearing system will net the transactions and debit X with 650 units (−900 + 250 = 650) against the total cash amount. This enables reduction of the number of movements and thus the costs.

Clearing organization   The clearing organization acts as the guarantor of the performance and settlement of contracts that are traded on an exchange.

Clearing system   System established to clear transactions.

Clearstream   CSD and clearing house based in Luxembourg and Frankfurt.

Closing day   In a new bond issue, the day when securities are delivered against payment by syndicate members participating in the offering.

Closing trade   A bought or sold trade which is used to partly offset an open position, to reduce it or to fully offset it and close it.

CMO   Central Moneymarkets Office – clearing house and depository for UK money markets.

Collateral   An acceptable asset used to cover a margin requirement.

Commercial paper   A money market instrument.

Commission   Charge levied by a firm for agency broking.

Commodity futures   These comprise five main categories; agriculturals (e.g. wheat and potatoes), softs (e.g. coffee and cocoa), precious metals (e.g. gold and silver), non-ferrous metals (e.g. copper and lead), and energies (e.g. oil and gas).

Common stock   Securities which represent ownership in a corporation. The two most important common stockholder rights are the voting right and dividend right. Common stockholder's claims on corporate assets are subordinate to those of bondholders preferred stockholders and general creditors.

Compliance officer   Person appointed within an authorized firm to be responsible for ensuring compliance with the rules.

Compound interest   Interest calculated on the assumption that interest amounts will be received periodically and can be reinvested (usually at the same rate).

Conduct of Business Rules Rules required by FSA 1986 to dictate how firms conduct their business. They deal mainly with the relationship between firm and client.

Conflicts of interest Circumstances that arise where a firm has an investment which could encourage it not to treat its clients favourably. The more areas in which a firm is involved, the greater the number of potential conflicts.

Confirm An agreement for each individual OTC transaction which has specific terms.

Continuous net settlement Extends multilateral netting to handle failed trades brought forward. *See **Multilateral netting***.

Contract The standard unit of trading for futures and options. It is also commonly referred to as a 'lot'.

Contract for difference Contract designed to make a profit or avoid a loss by reference to movements in the price of an item. The underlying item cannot change hands.

Contract note Legal documentation sent by securities house to clients providing details of a transaction completed on their behalf.

Conversion premium The effective extra cost of buying shares through exercising a convertible bond compared with buying the shares directly in the market. Usually expressed as percentage of the current market price of the shares.

Conversion price The normal value of a convertible which may be exchanged for one share.

Conversion ratio The number of shares into which a given amount (e.g. £100 or $1000) of the nominal value of a convertible can be converted.

Convertible bond Security (usually a bond or preferred stock) that can be exchanged for other securities, usually common stock of the same issuer, at the option of the holder and under certain conditions.

Convertible currency A currency that is freely convertible into another currency. Currencies for which domestic exchange control legislation specifically allows conversion into other currencies.

Corporate action One of many possible capital restructuring changes or similar actions taken by the company, which may have an impact on the market price of its securities, and which may require the shareholders to make certain decisions.

Corporate debt securities   Bonds or commercial papers issued by private corporations.

Correlation   Refers to the degree to which fluctuations of one variable are similar to those of another.

Cost of carry   The net running cost of holding a position (which may be negative), e.g. the cost of borrowing cash to buy a bond, less the coupon earned on the bond while holding it.

Counterparty   A trade can take place between two or more counterparties. Usually one party to a trade refers to its trading partners as counterparties.

Coupon   Generally, the nominal annual rate of interest expressed as a percentage of the principal value. The interest is paid to the holder of a fixed income security by the borrower. The coupon is generally paid annually, semi-annually or, in some cases quarterly depending on the type of security.

Credit risk   The risk that a borrower, or a counterparty to a deal, or the issuer of a security, will default on repayment or not deliver its side of the deal.

CREST   The organization in the UK that holds UK and Irish company shares in dematerialized form and clears and settles trades in UK and Irish company shares.

CRESTCo   Organization which owns CREST.

CREST member   A participant within CREST who holds stock in stock accounts in CREST and whose name appears on the share register. A member is their own *user*.

CREST sponsored member   A participant within CREST who holds stock in stock accounts in CREST and whose name appears on the share register. Unlike a member, a sponsored member is not their own user. The link to CREST is provided by another user who sponsors the sponsored member.

CREST user   A participant within CREST who has an electronic link to CREST.

Cross-border trading   Trading which takes place between persons or entities from different countries.

Cum-dividend With dividend.

Cumulative preference share If the company fails to pay a preference dividend the entitlement to the dividend accumulates and the arrears of preference dividend must be paid before any ordinary dividend.

Currency exposure Currency exposure exists if assets are held or income earned, in one currency while liabilities are denominated in another currency. The position is exposed to changes in the relative values of the two currencies such that the cost of the liabilities may be increased or the value of the assets or earning decreased.

CUSIP The committee on Uniform Securities Identification Procedures, the body which established a consistent securities numbering system in the United States.

Custodian Institution holding securities in safekeeping for a client. A custodian also offers different services to its clients (settlement, portfolio services, etc.)

Customer-non-private Customer who is assumed to understand the workings of the investment world and therefore receives little protection from the Conduct of Business Rules.

Customer-private Customer who is assumed to be financially unsophisticated and therefore receives more protection from the Conduct of Business Rules.

Day count fraction The proportion of a year by which an interest rate is multiplied in order to calculate the amount accrued or payable.

Dealer Individual or firm that acts as principal in all transactions, buying for their own account.

Default Failure to perform on a futures contract, either cash settlement or physical settlement.

Deliverable basket The list of securities which meets the delivery standards of futures contracts.

Delivery The physical movement of the underlying asset on which the derivative is based from seller to buyer.

Delivery versus payment Settlement where transfer of the security and payment for that security occur simultaneously.

Dematerialized (form) Circumstances where securities are held in a book entry transfer system with no certificates.

Depository receipts   Certificate issued by a bank in a country to represent shares of a foreign corporation issued in a foreign country. It entitles the holder to dividends and capital gains. They trade and pay dividend in the currency of the country of issuance of the certificate.

Depository Trust Company (DTC)   A US central securities depository through which members may arrange deliveries of securities between each other through electronic debit and credit entries without the physical delivery of the securities. DTC is industry-owned with the NYSE as the majority owner and is a member of the Federal Reserve System.

Derivative   A financial instrument whose value is dependent upon the value of an underlying asset.

Dirty price   The total price of a bond including accrued interest.

Disclaimer   A notice or statement intending to limit or avoid potential legal liability.

Deutsche Börse   The German Stock Exchange.

Dividend   Distribution of profits made by a company if it chooses to do so.

Dividend per share   Indicated annual dividend based on the most recently announced quarterly dividend times four plus any additional dividends to be paid during the current fiscal year.

Dividend yield   The dividend expressed as a percentage of the share price.

DK   Don't Know. Applies to a securities transaction pending settlement where fundamental data are missing which prevents the receiving party from accepting delivery.

Domestic bond   Bond issued in the country of the issuer, in its country and according to the regulations of that country.

DTC   Depository Trust Company – CSD for shares in the USA.

ECB   European Central Bank.

ECSDA   European Central Securities Depository Association.

EFP   Exchange of futures for physical. Common in the energy markets. A physical deal priced on the futures markets.

EUCLID   Communications system operated by Euroclear.

EUREX German–Swiss derivatives exchange created by the merger of the German (DTB) and Swiss (SOFFEX) exchanges.

EURONEXT A Pan-European exchange incorporating the Dutch, French, Portuguese and Belgium Exchanges and LIFFE.

Earnings per share (EPS) The total profit of a company divided by the number of shares in issue.

Equity A common term to describe stocks or shares.

Equity/stock options Contracts based on individual equities or shares. On exercise of the option the specified amount of shares are exchanged between the buyer and the seller through the clearing organization.

E-T-D This is the common term which is used to describe exchange-traded derivatives which are the standardized products. It also differentiates products which are listed on an exchange as opposed to those offered Over-The-Counter.

EURIBOR A measure of the average cost of funds over the whole euro area based on a panel of 57 banks.

Eurobond An interest-bearing security issued across national borders, usually issued in a currency other than that of the issuer's home country.

Euroclear A book-entry clearing facility for most Eurocurrency and foreign securities. It is linked to EURONEXT.

European style option An option which can only be exercised on the expiry day.

Exception-based processing Transaction processing where straightforward items are processed automatically, allowing staff to concentrate on the items which are incorrect or not straightforward.

Execution and clearing agreement An agreement signed between the client and the clearing broker. This agreement sets out the terms by which the clearing broker will conduct business with the client.

Exchange Marketplace for trading.

Exchange delivery settlement price (EDSP) The price determined by the exchange for physical delivery of the underlying instrument or cash settlement.

Exchange-owned clearing organization Exchange- or member-owned clearing organizations are structured so that the clearing members each guarantee each other with the use of a members' default fund and additional funding such as insurance, with no independent guarantee.

Exchange rate The rate at which one currency can be exchanged for another.

Ex-date Date on or after which a sale of securities is executed without the right to receive dividends or other entitlements.

Ex-dividend Thirty-seven days before interest payment is due gilt-edged stocks are made 'ex-dividend'. After a stock has become 'ex-dividend', a buyer of stock purchases it without the right to receive the next (pending) interest payment.

Execution The action of trading in the markets.

Execution and clearing agreement An agreement signed between the client and the clearing broker. This sets out the terms by which the clearing broker will conduct business with the client.

Execution only or give-up agreement Tripartite agreement which is signed by the executing broker, the clearing broker and the client. This sets out the terms by which the clearing broker will accept business on behalf of the client.

Exercise The process by which the holder of an option may take up their right to buy or sell the underlying asset.

Exercise price (or strike price) The fixed price, per share or unit, at which an option conveys the right to call (purchase) or put (sell) the underlying shares or units.

Expiry date The last date on which an option holder can exercise their right. After this date an option is deemed to lapse or be abandoned.

Face value The value of a bond, note, mortgage or other security that appears on the face of the issue, unless the value is otherwise specified by the issuing company. Face value is ordinarily the amount the issuing company promises to pay at maturity. It is also referred to as par or nominal value.

Failed transaction A securities transaction that does not settle on time; i.e. the securities and/or cash are not exchanged as agreed on the settlement date.

Final settlement The completion of a transaction when the delivery of all components of a trade is performed.

Financial futures/options contracts Financial futures is a term used to describe futures contracts based on financial instruments such as currencies, debt instruments and financial indices.

Financial Services Authority (FSA) The agency designated by the Treasury to regulate investment business as required by FSA 1986 and then FSMA 2000. It is the main regulator of the financial sector and was formerly called the Securities and Investments Board (SIB). It assumed its full powers on 1 December 2001.

First notice day The first day that the holders of short positions can give notification to the exchange/clearing house that they wish to effect delivery.

Fiscal agent A commercial bank appointed by the borrower to undertake certain duties related to the new issue, such as assisting the payment of interest and principal, redeeming bonds or coupons, handling taxes, replacement of lost or damaged securities, destruction of coupons and bonds once payments have been made.

Fixed income Interest on a security which is calculated as a constant specified percentage of the principal amount and paid at the end of specified interest periods, usually annually or semi-annually, until maturity.

Fixed rate A borrowing or investment where the interest or coupon paid is fixed throughout the arrangement. In a FRA or coupon swap, the fixed rate is the fixed interest rate paid by one party to the other, in return for a floating-rate receipt (i.e. an interest rate that is to be refixed at some future time or times).

Fixed-rate borrowing This establishes the interest rate that will be paid throughout the life of the loan.

Flat position A position which has been fully closed out and no liability to make or take delivery exists.

Floating rate A borrowing or investment where the interest or coupon paid changes throughout the arrangement in line with some reference rate such as LIBOR. In a FRA or coupon swap, the floating rate is the floating interest rate (i.e. an interest rate that is to be refixed at some future time or times) paid by one party to the other, in return for a fixed-rate receipt.

Floating-rate note (FRN)   Bond where each interest payment is made at the current or average market levels, often by reference to LIBOR.

Foreign bond   Bond issued in a domestic market in the domestic currency and under the domestic rules of issuance by a foreign issuer (ex. Samurai bonds are bonds issued by issuers of other countries on the Japanese market).

Forex   Abbreviation for foreign exchange (currency trading).

Forward delivery   Transactions which involve a delivery date in the future.

Forward-rate agreements (FRAs)   An agreement where the client can fix the rate of interest that will be applied to a notional loan or deposit, drawn or placed on an agreed date in the future, for a specified term.

Forwards   These are very similar to futures contracts but they are not mainly traded on an exchange. They are not marked to market daily but settled only on the delivery date.

FSA   Financial Services Authority.

FT-SE 100 index   Main UK share index based on 100 leading shares.

Fund manager   An organization that invests money on behalf of someone else.

Futures   An agreement to buy or sell an asset at a certain time in the future for a certain price.

Gearing   The characteristic of derivatives which enables a far greater reward for the same, or much smaller, initial outlay. It is the ratio of exposure to investment outlay, and is also known as leverage.

Gilt   Domestic sterling-denominated long-term bond backed by the full faith and credit of the UK and issued by the Treasury.

Gilt-edged market-makers (GEMMs)   A firm that is a market maker in gilts. Also known as a primary dealer.

Gilt-edged security   UK government borrowing.

Give-up   The process of giving a trade to a third party who will undertake the clearing and settlement of the trade.

Global clearing The channelling of the settlement of all futures and options trades through a single counterparty or through a number of counterparties geographically located.

Global custodian Institution that safekeeps, settles and performs processing of income collection, tax reclaim, multicurrency reporting, cash management, foreign exchange, corporate action and proxy monitoring etc. for clients' securities in all required marketplaces.

Global depository receipt (GDR) A security representing shares held in custody in the country of issue.

Good delivery Proper delivery of certificates that are negotiable and complete in terms of documentation or information.

Gross A position which is held with both the bought and sold trades kept open.

GSCC Government Securities Clearing Corporation – clearing organization for US Treasury securities.

Guaranteed bond Bonds on which the principal or income or both are guaranteed by another corporation or parent company in case of default by the issuing corporation.

Haircut The discount applied to the value of collateral used to cover margins.

Hedging A trading method which is designed to reduce or mitigate risk. Reducing the risk of a cash position in the futures instrument to offset the price movement of the cash asset. A broader definition of hedging includes using futures as a temporary substitute for the cash position.

Holder A person who has bought an open derivatives contract.

Immobilization The storage of securities certificates in a vault in order to eliminate physical movement of certificates/documents in transfer of ownership.

Independent clearing organization The independent organization is quite separate from the actual members of the exchange, and will guarantee to each member the performance of the contracts by having them registered in the organization's name.

Initial margin The deposit which the clearing house calls as protection against a default of a contract. It is returnable to the clearing member once the position is closed. The level is subject to changes in line with market conditions.

Institutional investor An institution which is usually investing money on behalf of others. Examples are mutual funds and pension funds.

Interest rate futures Based on a debt instrument such as a government bond or a Treasury bill as the underlying product and require the delivery of a bond or bill to fulfil the contract.

Interest rate swap An agreement to exchange interest related payments in the same currency from fixed rate into floating rate (or vice versa) or from one type of floating rate to another.

Interim dividend Dividend paid part-way through a year in advance of the final dividend.

International depository receipt (IDR) Receipt of shares of a foreign corporation held in the vaults of a depository bank. The receipt entitles the holder to all dividends and capital gains. Dividends and capital gains are converted to local currency as part of the service. IDRs allow investors to purchase foreign shares without having to involve themselves in foreign settlements and currency conversion.

International equity An equity of a company based outside the UK but traded internationally.

International petroleum exchange (IPE) Market for derivatives of petrol and oil products.

International securities identification number (ISIN) A coding system developed by the ISO for identifying securities. ISINs are designated to create one unique worldwide number for any security. It is a 12-digit alphanumeric code.

Interpolation The estimation of a price or rate, usually for a broken date, from two other rates or prices, each of which is for a date either side of the required date.

Intra-day margin An extra margin call which the clearing organization can call during the day when there is a very large movement up or down in the price of the contract.

Intrinsic value The amount by which an option is in-the-money.

Investment services directive (ISD) European Union Directive imposing common standards on investment business.

Investments Items defined in the FSA 1986 to be regulated by it. Includes shares, bonds, options, futures, life assurance and pensions.

Invoice amount The amount calculated under the formula specified by the futures exchange which will be paid in settlement of the delivery of the underlying asset.

IOSCO International Organization of Securities Commissions.

IPMA International Primary Markets Association.

Irredeemable gilt A gilt with no fixed date for redemption. Investors receive interest indefinitely.

ISDA International Swaps and Derivatives Association, previously known as the International Swap Dealers Association. Many market participants use ISDA documentation.

ISMA International Securities Markets Association.

ISSA The International Securities Services Association.

Issuer Legal entity that issues and distributed securities.

Issuing agent Agent (e.g. bank) who puts original issues out for sale.

JASDEC Japan Securities Depository Centre – the CSD for Japan.

JSCC Japan Securities Clearing Corporation – clearing organization in Japan.

Last notice day The final day that notification of delivery of a futures contract will be possible. On most exchanges all outstanding short futures contracts will be automatically delivered to open long positions.

Last trading day Often the day preceding last notice day which is the final opportunity for holders of long positions to trade out of their positions and avoid ultimate delivery.

LCH London Clearing House.

Leverage The magnification of gains and losses by only paying for part of the underlying value of the instrument or asset; the smaller the amount of funds invested, the greater the leverage. It is also known as gearing.

LIBID The London inter-bank bid rate. The rate at which one bank will lend to another.

LIBOR The London inter-bank offered rate. It is the rate used when one bank borrows from another bank. It is the benchmark used to price many capital market and derivative transactions.

LIFFE London International Financial Futures and Options Exchange.

Liquidity A liquid asset is one that can be converted easily and rapidly into cash without a substantial loss of value. In the money market, a security is said to be liquid if the spread between bid and asked price is narrow and reasonable size can be done at those quotes.

Liquidity risk The risk that a bank may not be able to close out a position because the market is illiquid.

Listed securities Securities listed on a stock exchange are tradeable on this exchange.

Loan stock *See* **Bonds**.

London Inter-Bank Offer Rate (LIBOR) Rate at which banks lend to each other which is often used as the benchmark for floating rate loans (FRNs).

London International Financial Futures and Options Exchange (LIFFE) Market for trading in bond, interest rate, FT-SE 100 index and FT-SE Mid 250 index, futures, plus equity options and soft commodity derivatives.

London Metal Exchange (LME) Market for trading in derivatives of metals such as copper, tin, zinc, etc.

London Stock Exchange (LSE) Market for trading in securities. Formerly know as the International Stock Exchange of the UK and Republic of Ireland or ISE.

Long A bought position in a derivative which is held open.

Long-dated Gilts with more than 15 years until redemption.

Long position Refers to an investor's account in which he has more shares of a specific security than he needs to meet his settlement obligations.

Lot The common term used to describe the standard unit of trading for futures and options. It is also referred to as a 'contract'.

Mandatory event   A corporate action which affects the securities without giving any choice to the security holder.

Margin   *Initial margin* is collateral placed by one party with a counterparty or clearing house at the time of a deal, against the possibility that the market price will move against the first party, thereby leaving the counterparty with a credit risk. *Variation margin* is a payment made, or collateral transferred, from one party to the other because the market price of the transaction or of collateral has changed. Variation margin payment is either in effect a settlement of profit/loss (for example, in the case of a futures contract) or the reduction of credit exposure. In a loan, margin is the extra interest above a benchmark such as LIBOR required by a lender to compensate for the credit risk of that particular borrower.

Mark-to-market   The process of revaluing an OTC or exchange-traded product each day. It is the difference between the closing price on the previous day against the current closing price. For exchange traded products this is referred to as variation margin.

Market   Description of any organization or facility through which items are traded. All exchanges are markets.

Market counterparty   A person dealing as agent or principal with the broker and involved in the same nature of investment business as the broker. This also includes fellow members of the FSA or trading members of an investment exchange for those products only where they are members.

Market-maker   A trader who works for an organization such as an investment bank. They quote bids and offers in the market and are normally under an obligation to make a price in a certain number of contracts. They create liquidity in the contract by offering to buy or sell.

Market price   In the case of a security, the market price is usually considered as the last reported price at which the stock or bond has been sold.

Market risk   Also position risk. The risk that the market value of a position falls.

Market value   The price at which a security is trading and could presumably be purchased or sold.

Master agreement This agreement is for OTC transactions and is signed between the client and the broker. It covers the basic terms under which the client and broker wish to transact business. Each individual trade has a separate individual agreement with specific terms known as a confirm.

Matching (comparison) Another term for comparison (or checking); a matching system to compare trades and ensure that both sides of trade correspond.

Maturity The date on which the principal or nominal value of a bond becomes due and payable in full to the holder.

Medium dated Gilts due to be redeemed within the next seven to fifteen years.

Model risk The risk that the computer model used by a bank for valuation or risk assessment is incorrect or misinterpreted.

Modified following The convention that if a settlement date in the future falls on a non-business day, the settlement date will be moved to the next following business day, unless this moves it to the next month, in which case the settlement date is moved back to the last previous business day.

Money market The market for the purchase and sale of short-term financial instruments. Short term is usually defined as less than one year.

Money rate of return Annual return as a percentage of asset value.

MOF The Ministry of Finance (Japan).

Multilateral netting Trade between several counterparties in the same security are netted such that each counterparty makes only one transfer of cash or securities to another party or to a central clearing system. Handles only transactions due for settlement on the same day.

Mutual collateralization The deposit of collateral by both counterparties to a transaction.

NASDAQ National Association of Securities Dealers Automated Quotation system.

Netting Trading partners offset their positions thereby reducing the number of positions for settlement. Netting can be *bilateral, multilateral* or *continuous net settlement*.

Net asset value (NAV) In mutual funds, the market value of the fund share. It is common practice for an investment trust to compute its assets daily, or even twice a day, by totalling the closing market value of all securities and assets (i.e. cash) owned. All liabilities are deducted, and the balance is divided by the number of shares outstanding. The resulting figure is the net asset value per share.

Net present value (NPV) The net total of several present values (arising from cashflows at different future dates) added together, some of which may be positive and some negative.

Nil paid rights price Ex-rights price less the subscription price.

Nominal amount Value stated on the face of a security (principal value, par value). Securities processing: number of securities to deliver/receive.

Nominal value of a bond The value at which the capital, or principal, of a bond will be redeemed by the issuer. Also called par value.

Nominal value of a share The minimum price at which a share can be issued. Also called par value.

Nominee An organization that acts as the named owner of securities on behalf of a different beneficial owner who remains anonymous to the company.

Non-callable Cannot be redeemed by the issuer for a stated period of time from date of issue.

Non-clearing member A member of an exchange who does not undertake to settle their derivatives business. This type of member must appoint a clearing member to register all their trades at the clearing organization.

Non-cumulative preference share If the company fails to pay a preference dividend the entitlement to the dividend is simply lost. There is no accumulation.

Non-private customer A person who is not a private customer or who has requested to be treated as a non-private customer.

Nostro reconciliation Checking the entries shown on the bank's nostro account statement with the bank's internal records (the accounting ledgers) to ensure that they correspond exactly.

Note   Bonds issued with a relatively short maturity are often called notes.

Notional   Contracts for differences require a notional principal amount on which settlement can be calculated.

Novation   The process where registered trades are cancelled with the clearing members and substituted by two new ones – one between the clearing house and the clearing member seller, the other between the clearing house and the clearing member buyer.

NSCC   National Securities Clearing Corporation – clearing organization for US shares.

OASYS   Trade confirmation system for US brokers operated by Thomson Financial Services.

Obligation netting   An arrangement to transfer only the net amount (of cash or a security) due between two or more parties, rather than transfer all amounts between the parties on a gross basis.

Off-balance sheet   A transaction whose principal amount is not shown on the balance sheet because it is a contingent liability or settled as a contract for differences.

Offer price   The price at which a trader or market-maker is willing to sell a contract.

Offshore   Relates to locations outside the controls of domestic monetary, exchange and legislative authorities. Offshore may not necessarily be outside the national boundaries of a country. In some countries, certain banks or other institutions may be granted offshore status and thus be exempt from all or specific controls or legislation.

Omnibus account   Account containing the holdings of more than one client.

On-balance sheet   A transaction whose principal amount is shown on the balance sheet.

On-line   Processing which is executed via an interactive input onto a PC or stationary terminal connected to a processing centre.

Open outcry   The style of trading whereby traders face each other in a designated area such as a pit and shout or call their respective bids and offers. Hand signals are also used to communicate. It is governed by exchange rules.

Open interest The number of contracts both bought and sold which remain open for delivery on an exchange. Important indicator for liquidity.

Open position The number of contracts which have not been off set at the clearing organization by the close of business.

Opening trade A bought or sold trade which is held open to create a position.

Operational risk The risk of losses resulting from inadequate systems and control, human errors or management failings.

Option An option is in the case of the *buyer*; the right, but not the obligation, to take (call) or make (put) for delivery of the underlying product and in the case of the *seller*; the obligation to make or take delivery of the underlying product.

Option premium The sum of money paid by the buyer for acquiring the right of the option. It is the sum of money received by the seller for incurring the obligation, having sold the rights, of the option. It is the sum of the intrinsic value and the time value.

Optional dividend Dividend that can be paid either in cash or in stock. The shareholders entitled to the dividend make the choice.

Options on futures These have the same characteristics as an option, the difference being that the underlying product is either a long or short futures contract. Premium is not exchanged, the contracts are marked to market each day.

Order-driven market A stock market where brokers acting on behalf of clients match trades with each other either on the trading floor of the exchange or through a central computer system.

Out-of-pocket expenses Market charges which are charged to the client without taking any profit.

Out-trade A trade which has been incorrectly matched on the floor of an exchange.

Over-the-counter (OTC) A one-to-one agreement between two counterparties where the specifications of the product are completely flexible and non-standardized.

Over-the-counter trading Trading made outside a stock exchange.

Pair off   Back-to-back trade between two parties where settlement occurs only by exchanging the cash difference between the two parties.

Par value   *See* **Nominal value**.

Pari passu   Without partiality. Securities that rank *pari passu*, rank equally with each other.

Paying agent   A bank which handles payment of interest and dividends on behalf of the issuer of a security.

Payment date   Date on which a dividend or an interest payment is scheduled to be paid.

Perpetual bond   A bond which has no redemption date.

Portfolio   List of investments held by an individual or company, or list of loans made by a bank or financial institution.

Premium   An option premium is the amount paid upfront by the purchaser of the option to the writer.

Present value   The amount of money which needs to be invested (or borrowed) now at a given interest rate in order to achieve exactly a given cashflow in the future, assuming compound reinvestment (or refunding) of any interest payments received (or paid) before the end. *See* **Future value**.

Pre-settlement   Checks and procedures undertaken immediately after execution of a trade prior to settlement.

Principal protected product   An investment whose maturity value is guaranteed to be at least the principal amount invested initially.

Principal-to-principal market   A market where the clearing house recognizes only the clearing member as one entity, and not the underlying clients of the clearing member.

Principal trading   When a member firm of the London Stock Exchange buys stock from or sells stock to a non-member.

Principal value   That amount inscribed on the face of a security and exclusive of interest or premium. It is the one used in the computation of interest due on such a security.

Private customer   An individual person who is not acting in the course of carrying on investment business.

Proprietary trader   A trader who deals for an organization such as an investment bank taking advantage of short-term price movements as well as taking long-term views on whether the market will move up or down.

Put option An option that gives the buyer the right, but not the obligation, to sell a specified quantity of the underlying asset at a fixed price, on or before a specified date. The seller of a put option has the obligation (because they have sold the right) to take delivery of the underlying asset if the option is exercised by the buyer.

Quote driven Dealing system where some firms accept the responsibility to quote buying and selling prices.

Range forward A forward outright with two forward rates, where settlement takes place at the higher forward rate if the spot rate at maturity is higher than that, at the lower forward rate if the spot rate at maturity is lower than that, or at the spot rate at maturity otherwise.

RCH Recognized clearing house under FSMA 2000.

Real-time gross settlement (RTGS) Gross settlement system where trades are settled continuously through the processing day.

Realized profit Profit which has arisen from a real sale.

Recognized investment exchange (RIE) Status required by FSMA 2000 for exchanges in the UK.

Reconciliation The comparison of a person's records of cash and securities position with records held by another party and the investigation and resolution of any discrepancies between the two sets of records.

Record date The date on which a securities holder must hold the securities in order to receive an income or entitlement.

Redemption The purchase and cancellation of outstanding securities through a cash payment to the holder.

Redemption price A price at which bonds may be redeemed, or called, at the issuer's option, prior to maturity (often with a slight premium).

Registered bond A bond whose owner is registered with the issuer or its registrar.

Registered title Form of ownership of securities where the owner's name appears on a register maintained by the company.

Registrar An official of a company who maintains its share register.

Registrar of companies   Government department responsible for keeping records of all companies.

Replacement cost   The mark-to-market loss which would be incurred if it were necessary to undertake a new transaction to replace an existing one, because the existing counterparty defaulted.

Repurchase agreement (repo)   Borrowing funds by providing a government security for collateral and promising to 'repurchase' the security at the end of the agreed upon time period. The associated interest rate is the 'repo-rate'.

Reputational risk   The risk that an organization's reputation will be damaged.

RIE   Recognized investment exchange under FSA 1986.

Rights issue   Offer of shares made to existing shareholders.

Right of offset   Where positions and cash held by the clearing organization in different accounts for a member are allowed to be netted.

Risk warning   Document that must be despatched and signed by private customers before they deal in traded options.

Roll-over   A LIBOR fixing on a new tranche of loan, or transfer of a futures position to the next delivery month.

Rolling settlement   System used in most countries including England. Bargains are settled a set number of days after being transacted.

Safekeeping   Holding of securities on behalf of clients. They are free to sell at any time.

SCL   Settlement organization and custodian of Spanish securities.

Scrip dividends   Scrip dividends options provide shareholders with the choice of receiving dividend entitlements in the form of cash, share or a combination or both. The amount of stocks to be distributed under a scrip option is calculated by dividing the cash dividend amount by the average market price over a recent period of time.

Scrip issue   *See* **Bonus issue**.

SEATS Plus   An order-driven system used on the London Stock Exchange for securities which do not attract at least two firms of market-makers and for all AIM securities.

Secondary market   Marketplace for trading in existing securities. The price at which they are trading has no direct effect on the company's fortunes but is a reflection of investors' perceptions of the company.

Securities   Bonds and equities.

Securities house   General term covering any type of organization involved in securities although usually reserved for the larger firms.

Securities lending   Loan of securities by an investor to another (usually a broker-dealer), usually to cover a short sale.

Securities and futures authority (SFA)   Prior to the FSA assuming its full powers, it was the SRO responsible for regulating securities and futures firms.

Securities and investments board (SIB)   Former name of the Financial Services Authority.

SEDOL   Stock Exchange Daily Official List, a securities numbering system assigned by the International Stock Exchange in London.

Segregated account   Account in which there is only the holdings of one client.

Segregation of funds   Where the client assets are held separately from those assets belonging to the member firm.

Self-regulating organizations (SROs)   Bodies which receive their status from FSA and are able to regulate sectors of the financial services industry. Membership of an SRO provides authorization.

SEQUAL   The checking system used for international equities.

SETS   London Stock Exchange Trading System.

Settlement   The fulfilment of the contractual commitments of transacted business.

Settlement date   The date on which a trade is cleared by delivery of securities against funds (actual settlement date, contractual settlement date).

Share option   A right sold to an investor conferring the option to buy or sell shares of a particular company at a predetermined price and within a specified time limit.

Short   A sold position in a derivative which is held open.

Short coupons   Bonds or notes with a short current maturity.

Short cover   The purchase of a security that has been previously sold short. The purpose is to return securities that were borrowed to make a delivery.

Short-dated gilt   Gilts due to be redeemed within the next seven years, according to the LSE (FT states up to 5 years).

Short sale   The sale of securities not owned by the seller in the expectation that the price of these securities will fall or as part of an arbitrage.

Short selling   Selling stock that you do not own.

Short-term security   Generally an obligation maturing in less than one year.

SICOVAM   CSD for French corporate securities and OATs (now merged with Euroclear).

Simple interest   Interest calculated on the assumption that there is no opportunity to re-invest the interest payments during the life of an investment and thereby earn extra income.

SIS   SEGA Inter Settle – CSD for Switzerland.

Soft commodities   Description given to commodities such as sugar, coffee and cocoa, traded through LIFFE since its incorporation of the former London Commodity Exchange (LCE).

Sovereign debt securities   Bonds issued by the government of a country.

SPAN   Standardized Portfolio Analysis of Risk. A form of margin calculation which is used by various clearing organizations.

Speculation   A deal undertaken because the dealer expects prices to move in his favour and thereby realize a profit.

Speculator   The speculator is a trader who wants to assume risk for potentially much higher rewards.

Sponsored member   Type of CREST member whose name appears on the register but has no computer link with CREST.

Spot delivery   A delivery or settlement of currencies on the value date, two business days later.

Spot market   Market for immediate as opposed to future delivery. In the spot market for foreign exchange, settlement is in two business days ahead.

Spot month   The first month for which futures contracts are available.

Spot rate   The price prevailing in the spot market.

Spread   (1) The difference between bid and asked price on a security. (2) Difference between yield on or prices of two securities of different types or maturities. (3) In underwriting, difference between price realized by an issuer and price paid by the investor. (4) Difference between two prices or two rates. What commodities traders would refer to as the basis.

Stamp duty   Tax on purchase of equities in the UK.

Stamp Duty Reserve Tax (SDRT) (UK)   Tax payable on the purchase of UK equities in uncertified form (i.e. those held within CREST).

Standard settlement instructions   Instructions for settlement with a particular counterparty which are always followed for a particular kind of deal and, once in place, are therefore not repeated at the time of each transaction.

Standing instruction   Default instruction, e.g. provided to an agent processing payments or clearing securities trades; provided by shareholder on how to vote shares (for example, vote for all management recommended candidates).

Stanza di compensazione   Italian clearing organization.

Stock   In some countries (e.g. the USA), the term applies to ordinary share capital of a company. In other countries (e.g. the UK), stock may mean share capital that is issued in variable amount instead of in fixed specified amounts, or it can describe government loans.

Stock dividend   Dividends paid by a company in stock instead of cash.

Stock Exchange Automated Quotation System (SEAQ)   Electronic screen display system through which market-makers in equities display prices at which they are willing to deal.

Stock Index Futures/Options   Based on the value of an underlying stock index such as the FTSE 100 in the UK, the S&P 500 index in the USA and the Nikkei 225 and 300 in Japan. Delivery is fulfilled by the payment or receipt of cash against the exchange calculated delivery settlement price. These are referred to as both indices or indexes.

Stock (order) An owner of a physical security that has been mutilated, lost or stolen will request the issuer to place a stop (transfer) on the security and to cancel and replace the security.

Stock (or bond) power A legal document, either on the back of registered stocks and bonds or attached to them, by which the owner assigns his interest in the corporation to a third party, allowing that party the right to substitute another name on the company records instead of the original owner's.

Stock split When a corporation splits its stock, it divides.

Straight debt A standard bond issue, without right to convert into the common shares of the issuer.

Straightthrough processing Computer transmission of the details of a trade, without manual intervention, from their original input by the trader to all other relevant areas – position keeping, risk control, accounts, settlement, reconciliation.

Street name Securities held in street name are held in the name of a broker or another nominee, i.e. a customer.

Strike price The fixed price, per share or unit, at which an option conveys the right to call (purchase) or put (sell) the underlying shares or units.

Strike price/rate Also exercise price. The price or rate at which the holder of an option can insist on the underlying transaction being fulfilled.

Stripped bonds (strips) Bonds where the rights to the interest payments and eventual repayment of the nominal value have been separated from each other and trade independently. Facility introduced for gilts in December 1997.

Sub-custodian A bank in a foreign country that acts on behalf of the custodian as its custody agent.

Subscription price Price at which shareholders of a corporation are entitled to purchase common shares in a rights offering or at which subscription warrants are exercisable.

Subscriptions In a bond issue, the buying orders from the lead manager, co-managers, underwriters and selling group members for the securities being offered.

Stump period   A calculation period, usually at the beginning or end of a swap, other than the standard ones normally quoted.

Swap   Arrangement where two borrowers, one of whom has fixed interest and one of whom has floating rate borrowings, swap their commitments with each other. A bank would arrange the swap and charge a fee.

SwapClear   A clearing house and central counterparty for swaps.

SwapsWire   An electronic dealing system for swaps.

SWIFT   Society for Worldwide Interbank Financial Telecommunications – secure electronic communications network between banks.

TARGET   Trans European Automated Real time Gross settlement Express Transfer – system linking the real-time gross settlements for euros in the 15 European Union countries.

Tax reclaim   The process that a global custodian and/or a holder of securities performs, in accordance with local government filing requirements, in order to recapture an allowable percentage of taxed withheld.

Termination date   The end date of a swap.

Thomson Report   An electronic transaction reporting system for international equities on the London Stock Exchange operated by Thomson.

Tick size   The value of a one-point movement in the contract price.

Time value   The amount by which an option's premium exceeds its intrinsic value. Where an option has no intrinsic value the premium consists entirely of time value.

Trade date   The date on which a trade is made.

Trade guarantees   Guarantees in place in a market which ensure that all compared or netted trades will be settled as compared regardless of a counterparty default.

Traded option   An option which is traded on an exchange.

Trader   An individual who buys and sells securities with the objective of making short-term gains.

Transfer agent   Agent appointed by a corporation to maintain records of stock and bond owners, to cancel and issue certificates and to resolve problems arising from lost, destroyed or stolen certificates.

Transfer form   Document which owners of registered documents must sign when they sell the security. Not required where a book entry transfer system is in use.

Transparency   The degree to which a market is characterized by prompt availability of accurate price and volume information which gives participants comfort that the market is fair.

TRAX   Trade confirmation system for the Euromarkets operated by ISMA.

Treasury bill   Money market instrument issued with a life of less than one year issued by the US and UK governments.

Treasury bonds (USA)   US government bond issued with a 30-year maturity.

Treasury notes (USA)   US government bond issued with 2-, 3-, 5- and 7-year maturity.

Triple A rating   The highest credit rating for a bond or company – the risk of default (or non-payment) is negligible.

Trustee   A person appointed to oversee the management of certain funds. They are responsible for ensuring that the fund is managed correctly and that the interests of the investor are protected and that all relevant regulations and legislation are complied with.

Turnaround   Securities bought and sold for settlement on the same day.

Turnaround time   The time available or needed to settle a turnaround trade.

Underlying asset   The asset from which the future or option's price is derived.

Undersubscribed   Circumstance when people have applied for fewer shares than are available in a new issue.

Unrealized profit   Profit which has not arisen from a sale – an increase in value of an asset.

Value at Risk (VaR)   The maximum amount which a bank expects to lose, with a given confidence level, over a given time period.

Variation margin   The process of revaluing an exchange-traded product each day. It is the difference between the closing price on the previous day against the current closing price. It is physically paid or received each day by the clearing organization. It is often referred to as the mark-to-market.

Volatility The degree of scatter of the underlying price when compared to the mean average rate.

Warrant An option which can be listed on an exchange, with a lifetime of generally more than one year.

Warrant agent A bank appointed by the issuer as an intermediary between the issuing company and the (physical) warrant holders, interacting when the latter want to exercise the warrants.

Withholding tax In the securities industry, a tax imposed by a government's tax authorities on dividends and interest paid.

Writer A person who has sold an open derivatives contract and is obliged to deliver or take delivery upon notification of exercise from the buyer.

XETRA Dealing system of the Deutsche Börse.

Yield Internal rate of return expressed as a percentage.

Yield curve For securities that expose the investor to the same credit risk, a graph showing the relationship at a given point in the time between yield and current maturity. Yield curves are typically drawn using yields on governments of various maturities.

Yield to maturity The rate of return yielded by a debt security held to maturity when both interest payments and the investor's capital gain or loss on the security are taken into account.

Zero coupon bond A bond issued with no coupon but a price substantially below par so that only capital is accrued over the life of the loan, and yield is comparable to coupon-bearing instruments.

Index

SECURITIES INSTITUTE

Qualifications

Securities Institute Diploma – the professional qualification for practitioners leading to Fellowship of the Institute

Investment Advice Certificate – the benchmark examination for financial advisors

SFA Registered Persons Examination – the benchmark examinations for employees of SFA regulated firms

Investment Administration Qualification – the benchmark examination for administration, operations and IT staff

International Capital Markets Qualification – the introductory qualification for overseas and emerging markets

Membership

Professionalism through a progressive structure of recognised designations: SIAff, MSI, FSI

Over 17,000 students, affiliates, members and fellows

Free membership events, providing education and networking opportunities

Examination qualification programmes

Continuing Learning opportunities through a wide range of courses and conferences with discounts available for members

Training, Continuing Learning & Publications for the financial services industry

The courses, seminars and publications we produce are researched and developed by working closely with market practitioners and employers to produce focussed, high quality and value-for-money training solutions that meet the needs of busy professionals.

To find out more about all our products and services, please call the Marketing Department on *020 7645 0670*, email us on *marketing@securities-institute.org.uk*, or visit our web site:

www.securities–institute.org.uk

Centurion House, 24 Monument Street, London, EC3R 8AQ

PROFESSIONALISM | INTEGRITY | EXCELLENCE